White-Collar Workers and the UAW

HD
6515
A8
S5,7

121921

White-Collar
Workers
and the UAW

Carl Dean Snyder

University of Illinois Press
Urbana, Chicago, London

GOSHEN COLLEGE LIBRARY
GOSHEN, INDIANA 46526

© 1973 by The Board of Trustees of the University of Illinois
Manufactured in the United States of America
Library of Congress Catalog Card No. 72–88954

ISBN 0–252–00286–5

to my Father and Mother
and the work crew at Black Lake—
Milly, Brad, Mark, and Marcia

Contents

Preface

One of the underlying dynamisms of American society is rapid technological change. Alvin Toffler's *Future Shock* suggests the possible scope and depth of accelerating technology's impact on individuals and social institutions.

My book examines only one ramification of this broad current. I am concerned here with the eroding action of technologically induced shifts in the composition of the labor force on those trade unions traditionally dependent upon blue-collar membership. Will the challenge posed by the massive drift toward the dominance of white-collar employees in the labor force be mastered by an effective union response? This is the vital question which unions are now forced to answer, either by affirmative actions or, negatively, by inaction and default.

If the answer is "yes"—and it now appears that this can be supported on the basis of overall white-collar membership gains of the last few years—will the new white-collar members be integrated, in part, within industrial union structures? Will they be organized into predominantly craft-like unions within the labor movement? Or will they constitute entirely autonomous "associations" unaffiliated with and isolated from the mainstream of organized labor?

The elements of one possible answer can be found in an examination of the International Union United Automobile, Aerospace, and Agricultural Implement Workers of America (called the UAW). A study of the white-collar experience of one of our largest industrial unions offers useful insights into the special problems of organizing, meeting the needs of, and servicing white-collar workers. This book examines the UAW during a crucial period of its white-collar history.

Particularly since 1957 this union has been formulating its unique answer to the white-collar challenge. Thus, here is a fifteen-year case study of a key industrial union's response to the problems arising from fundamental changes in the composition of the labor force within the industries of its jurisdiction. Supplemental documentary research extends this study back to the union's origins in the mid-1930's.

The developing experience of the UAW will determine an important part of the answer to the questions raised above. As one of the largest American unions, a leader among the industrial unions, and perhaps the primary innovating center of the labor movement, the UAW's victories and defeats in the white-collar field will extend an influence far beyond its own jurisdiction. An analysis of this union's specific program in the white-collar area will be the immediate focus of attention. But my broader concern throughout will be with those lessons learned from UAW experience which are general and, I believe, capable of application by other unions.

Beyond this loom still broader considerations. That white-collar workers be structured soundly into the society; that they have legitimated spokesmen who can effectively represent their unique interests and sensitive concerns in the sometimes chaotic contemporary scene; that they, like blue-collar workers, come to recognize their "stake in the system"—these considerations all may be of profound long-range importance to a society exposed to the unknown strains of onrushing technology. (It has been argued, for example, that a failure to integrate German white-collar workers into the total society was partly responsible for the rise of Hitler.)

By way of introduction to this consideration of the white-collar challenge and the UAW response, I will outline the overall direction of my analysis. The crux of the white-collar problem, from a union standpoint, is the special attitudes and characteristics of the white-collar employee himself. Here the literature of social science and personnel administration offers helpful generalizations. More immediately, I will use an interview study of white-collar autoworkers' attitudes.

The growth of the white-collar bloc and the evolving white-collar program of the UAW offers valuable instruction when examined historically. The Union has maintained many enduring, viable white-collar units over a thirty-year period. This alone constitutes a remarkable testimony to the stability and effectiveness of white-collar units within an industrial union. An outline of these developments since the early 1940's can be constructed from union documents and interview material.

An important part of this historical process was the slow crystallization of a white-collar interest group within the UAW. Eventually this became the Engineering-Technical-Office caucus (ETO). As an outgrowth of the activities of the caucus, the Office and Technical Department of the Union was fundamentally reconstituted in 1962 as the Technical-Office-Professional (TOP) Department. This new department has been a major source of the rebirth of UAW white-collar organizing.

The initiating role of the white-collar "rank-and-file" union member—now and in the future—must be examined in evaluating the possible impact of organization upon this part of the labor force. What kind of union member does the white-collar worker become? To what extent do his bargaining interests differ from those of production workers?

After examining the UAW's experience with white-collar organizing and membership, an agenda for other industrial unions can be usefully hazarded. What structures and activities need to be reexamined and modified in the typical industrial union? How fundamental are the changes required? What, ideally, would constitute a thorough-going renovation and reorientation of an industrial union toward white-collar effectiveness?

Finally, it is reasonable to speculate concerning the probable direction of development of unionism in the entire white-collar field. What does the UAW experience imply for the labor movement, for management, and for the economy? Will the political order and society as a whole be any different because of such organization?

My interest in the UAW dates back to 1948 and a seven-year period as an active blue-collar local union member and officer in one of the auto parts supplier firms. Roles included vice-president of the local union, president of the city CIO Council, education committee chairman, editor of the local labor newspaper, responsibility for a weekly radio program, and involvement in local labor political action. Subsequent enrollment in the interdisciplinary Doctor of Social Science program at the Maxwell School of Syracuse University helped provide the tools to more effectively understand and analyze that background of labor experience. Since 1957, I have personally followed the development of the UAW's white-collar effort as a continuing research interest.

Original interviewing began with staff personnel of the International UAW at Solidarity House in Detroit in 1958 and proceeded to the officers and active members of white-collar local unions and units in the Detroit area. A little later interviews were extended to management personnel. From this initial background, interview schedules were designed for inactive white-collar union members and for nonunion white-collar workers. A random sample technique was introduced in selecting these two groups.

Interview questions, in most instances, were phrased to elicit the freest possible response pattern. This meant that subsequently I had to categorize the answers. Interviews with management personnel tended to be limited to about an hour and to be conducted at their place of work. This was also true for staff personnel of the International UAW. Much more exhaustive discussions were possible with local union leaders. Interviews with other active members, inactive members, and nonunion white-collar workers were generally conducted at the interviewees' homes. These varied in duration from an infrequent minimum of one hour and a half to a frequent maximum of three to four hours.

Whatever value the present study possesses must be credited to contributions of time and patience by more than one hundred persons who shared my interest in the future of white-collar unionism.

Follow-up interviewing and contacts with key staff and white-collar members has continued down to the time of this writing. A highly valuable resource in this connection has been the opportunity to attend conferences of the UAW Technical-Office-Professional Advisory Councils.

Most immediately my appreciation goes to Douglas Fraser, vice-president of the International Union and director of the Technical-Office-Professional Department for Organizing. I am equally indebted to Wallace Webber, Hubert Emerick, Ray Sullivan, and Harold Schauer of the UAW staff and to many local union people at Locals 889, 412, and 212 for continuing contacts over the years.

The origin of the study can be credited to Professor Sidney Sufrin of the Maxwell School, and its practical implementation to Brendan Sexton, education director of the UAW. Professor W. Fred Cottrell of Miami University early stimulated my interest in the field of industrial sociology and, together with Professor Howard White, my involvement in interdisciplinary work.

Professor S. M. Miller should receive special recognition for his very useful interview instrument, which he made available to me at an early point in my investigation. This helped greatly in my own schedule construction.

Very practical assistance toward the time needed for reconsideration and revision of my work came from the grant of a sabbatical leave from Eastern Michigan University and the encouragement extended to me by Deans Albert Brown and Donald Drummond. I also appreciate the support and time made available to me by Professor Young-iob Chung. In addition Professor John Simpson deserves a special word of thanks for his continuing encouragement and assistance in seeking publication of the study. Needless to say, but important to record, is the fact that this book could not have been completed without the patience and support of my family.

An indispensable technical tool in the field of white-collar investigation first became available in 1957. I refer here to the *White-Collar Report,* published by the Bureau of National Affairs. This is without doubt the key reference source available for white-collar investigation. My numerous citations are an indication of its value.

Over the entire course of this study the helpful assistance of Mrs. Eleanor Scanlon Riegel of the University of Michigan's Bureau of Industrial Relations Library deserves a special word of appreciation.

In conclusion, I want to make clear that any criticism of the UAW implicit in portions of this discussion is intended entirely in a constructive spirit. I am much more persuaded by the overweighing, substantial successes of the Union in dealing with a highly intractable and complex problem than by some of the mistakes along the way.

Ever since my initial membership in the Union, I have been repeatedly impressed by the basic health, integrity, democracy, and dedication of the UAW as a whole. As a social scientist it is my view that the access which the UAW affords to the outside student of its affairs is exceeded by no other major institution in our society.

CARL DEAN SNYDER
Eastern Michigan University

White-Collar Workers and the UAW

Challenge
and
Response

1

An inherent characteristic of the maturation of industrial economies—as they develop larger production and administrative units, higher levels of technical complexity, varied service industries, and necessary governmental coordination—is the steady shift from blue-collar ("production") employment to white-collar jobs. These are the jobs covered by the U.S. Department of Labor's classification of "workers in clerical, professional, technical, sales and kindred occupations."[1]

In the United States from 1900 to 1960 the broad white-collar drift was demonstrated in the growth of white-collar employment from 28 percent to 47 percent of the nonfarm labor force. Most of this gain was at the expense of the blue-collar "share," which dropped from 57 percent in 1900 to less than 40 percent in 1960, while the "service workers" category remained nearly stable. The crossover point occurred in 1955. Since then there have been more white-collar workers than blue-collar workers in the American economy. The Bureau of Labor Statistics projects this trend to an estimated 51:33 ratio by 1980.[2]

[1] See Adolf Sturmthal, ed., *White-Collar Trade Unions* (Urbana: University of Illinois Press, 1966), pp. v, 367–374. Managers are also in this category but are typically ineligible for unionization.
[2] This trend slowed—temporarily, it appears—with the resurgence of American economic growth in the mid-1960's, along with the impact of the Vietnam war. See Everett Kassalow, "White-Collar Unionism in the United States," in Sturmthal, ed., *White-Collar Trade Unions*, p. 315. The long-term trends are documented in Carol Barry, "Special Labor Force Report," *Monthly Labor Review*, January, 1961, pp. 11–18, and David L. Kaplan and M. Clair Casey,

Occupational projections to 1980 for the particular white-collar groups with which I am here especially concerned (professional, technical, and clerical workers) also indicate a continued expansion.[3]

The white-collar drift has affected the manufacturing sector of the economy in somewhat the same way as it has the total economy. Particularly during the period of relative stagnation of economic growth in the late 1950's and early 1960's, industrial unions—such as the automobile workers, steel workers, and electrical workers—found their blue-collar base stable or declining, while the largely unorganized white-collar groups in their jurisdictions were steadily expanding. In each of the three industries of primary concern to the UAW—autos, aerospace, and agricultural implements—the white-collar group increased in relative importance.[4]

The "Lost Dynamic?"

In these same years the American labor movement came under extensive academic and intellectual criticism for a variety of alleged shortcomings.[5] A major item cited was organized labor's failure to maintain its relative position in the growing labor force. In 1953 some 34 percent of the nonfarm work force were union members. Yet in 1960 this percentage had fallen to 31.4 percent.[6] By 1966 it was 28.1 percent, and the most recent data available in 1971 indicated a 1968 figure of 27.9 percent. Since 1966 some improvement has been registered in terms of the

---

Occupational Trends in the United States, 1900 to 1950 (Washington, D.C.: Bureau of the Census, 1958). The 1980 projections are calculated from data in U.S. Department of Labor, *Manpower Report of the President* (Washington, D.C., 1971), p. 297.

[3] *Manpower Report, 1971,* p. 297.

[4] UAW, *Report of President Walter P. Reuther to the 16th Constitutional Convention, Atlantic City, New Jersey,* April 7-12, 1957, pp. 217–219.

[5] For a refutation and evaluation, see Brendan Sexton, "The Intellectuals and Trade Unions," *Proceedings of Sixteenth Annual Meeting* (Madison, Wis.: Industrial Relations Research Association, 1964), pp. 245–252.

[6] See U.S. Bureau of Labor Statistics, *Directory of National and International Labor Unions in the United States, 1961* (Washington, D.C.: U.S. Department of Labor, 1962), pp. 46–47.

percent organized of the total labor force. Statistics show an increase from 22.7 percent in 1966 to 23.0 percent in 1968.[7]

AFL-CIO Director of Organization William Kircher stated in 1967: "At the time of the AFL-CIO merger in December 1955, we thought in terms of perhaps 26 million unorganized workers and speculated that some 39 percent to 40 percent of the realistic potential was organized. Now, with 32 million constituting the organizing goal, we estimate that probably 35 percent of the realistic potential is in the labor movement."[8]

This failure to keep pace was frequently interpreted to be a measure of the lack of confidence of workers in the union institution. Some of the causal factors were, for a time, mutually reinforcing. The "tarnished image" of unionism failed to attract unorganized workers. On the other hand, the relative (and, at times, absolute) loss of members worked to confirm the intellectuals' analysis of stagnation or deterioration.

Whatever the specific, complex combination of factors responsible for this lag, it became increasingly clear that the largely unorganized white-collar sector did offer the possibility of recouping membership losses. For example, in 1957 the AFL-CIO pointed out that there were some 13 million potentially organizable white-collar workers outside the unions.[9]

Yet the overall union performance in white-collar organizing activity offered no refutation of the critics' thesis. Thus, while only 12 percent of American trade union members were white-collar employees in 1960, the net gain in this group by all unions between 1958 and 1960 was 8,000 members—or an increase of about 0.3 percent.[10] In contrast, the pick up in white-collar organizing following this low point resulted in its

[7] U.S. Bureau of Labor Statistics, *Directory of National and International Labor Unions in the United States, 1969* (Washington, D.C.: U.S. Department of Labor, 1970), p. 55.

[8] William L. Kircher, "Labor's Approach to the New Worker," *AFL-CIO American Federationist,* July, 1967, p. 4.

[9] John W. Livingston, "The Answer for the White-Collar Worker," in Industrial Union Department, AFL-CIO, *Labor Looks at the White-Collar Worker* (Washington, D.C.: Industrial Union Department, AFL-CIO, 1957), p. 64.

[10] U.S. Bureau of Labor Statistics, *Directory of Labor Unions, 1961,* p. 50.

increase to 14.4 percent of total union membership in 1964.[11] Between 1964 and 1966 white-collar membership increased by approximately 225,000, and its percent of total union membership increased to 14.7 percent. In 1968 3,176,000 white-collar workers were union members; they comprised 15.7 percent of all members. In the 1966–68 period white-collar union membership grew by 366,000; this represented over 33 percent of the total gain in union membership in that period. Thus we see the increasing relative importance of white-collar organizing.[12]

UAW Losses

UAW membership, which had peaked at 1,400,000 in 1953, had an irregular downward trend to a low of 1,000,000 in 1961. The Union's white-collar membership, cited at 80,000 in 1953, was estimated at 50,000 in 1963. Union officers during this period were estimating the white-collar organizing potential in their jurisdictions to be 250,000.[13]

In these years the Union appeared to be, at best, maintaining a holding action with its white-collar membership. UAW white-collar organizers and staff members, like those of other industrial unions, were highly pessimistic about the prospects for white-collar unionization.[14]

That the UAW's white-collar organizing program was "bogged down" is confirmed by the representation election summaries in

[11] Harry P. Cohany, "Trends and Changes in Union Membership," *Monthly Labor Review,* May, 1966, p. 511.

[12] U.S. Bureau of Labor Statistics, *Directory of Labor Unions, 1969,* p. 70.

[13] These are yearly average dues-paying membership data reported by Emil Mazey, International secretary-treasurer, in *UAW Solidarity.* The 1953 white-collar membership figure was cited in "It May Be Gone Forever," *Business Week,* November 6, 1954, pp. 64–71. The 1963 white-collar membership estimate is that of Benjamin K. Solomon and Robert K. Burns in "Unionization of White-Collar Employees: Extent, Potential, and Implications," *Journal of Business,* April, 1963, p. 146. The estimate of organizing potential was by Walter P. Reuther in Industrial Union Department, AFL-CIO, *Labor Looks at the White-Collar Worker,* pp. 3–4. In 1968, the Union estimated this potential to be 337,100 in the industries of its jurisdiction. See UAW, *Report of President Walter P. Reuther to the 21st Constitutional Convention, Atlantic City, N.J.,* May 4–10, 1968, p. 147.

[14] Interview data by author.

the Bureau of National Affairs' *White-Collar Report.* In 1961 the Union won two elections among white-collar employees for a total of 20 potential new members; it lost 11 elections for a total of 650 employees. This represented the low point in a trend extending from 1957—during those five years the UAW had won elections among a total of 915 employees.[15]

The implications of these trends were well expressed by the Union's vice-president, Leonard Woodcock, at the 1957 constitutional convention.

> I ask you to think what economic power will UAW have in these three great basic industries of the United States and Canada as we represent an increasingly smaller percentage of the total labor force. It is an inescapable fact that if we cannot achieve the organization of professional and technical and engineering employees, and also office workers, this union will become an increasingly less effective force.[16]

If unions were generally unsuccessful in the white-collar field, it would mean exclusion from the most dynamic, growing sector of the labor force as well.[17] This would certainly have adverse effects upon the long-term vitality of the labor movement in American life.

That "New White Collar"

In sharp contrast, the first ten months of 1967 saw the UAW win 34 elections among 2,250 white-collar employees, while losing 9 elections covering 710 workers. This was to be the best white-collar organizing year for the UAW since the early Chrysler victories. And in the previous year alone the Union had added more potential members than in the entire 1957–61 period.[18]

Despite the counteracting drain of the "erosion" of white-

---

[15] See Table 6–1, Ch. 6.

[16] See UAW, *Proceedings, 16th Constitutional Convention, Atlantic City, N.J.,* April 7–12, 1957, p. 280.

[17] Adolf Sturmthal, "White-Collar Unions—A Comparative Essay," in Sturmthal, ed., *White-Collar Trade Unions,* p. 375.

[18] Interview data by author. Also see *White-Collar Report,* no. 564, December 28, 1967, p. B-1.

collar bargaining units, total white-collar UAW membership has likewise begun to show a reversal of the 1957–61 trend. Existing units were estimated to include 88,362 members in 1971.[19]

This white-collar membership is strategically distributed across all three of the UAW's jurisdictions and is well located to serve as a base for future expansion. Thus the Union in 1966 had approximately 17,000 white-collar autoworkers, 27,500 such aerospace employees, and 3,000 white-collar agricultural implement members, with the remainder in related industries. The largest single concentration is 8,000 members at Chrysler, with other points of major strength at International Harvester and Curtiss-Wright.[20]

The changed UAW performance may reflect merely an improved trend for all unions in the economy. However, it should be noted that total white-collar union membership in all of manufacturing increased by only 11,000 between 1962 and 1964 —although there was a total gain of 300,000 white-collar union members in the entire economy.[21] Between 1964 and 1966 white-collar union membership in the economy increased by 159,000, yet in manufacturing a decrease of 16,000 was recorded.[22] However, in these latter two years the UAW won bargaining rights for at least 1,926 employees in National Labor Relations Board (NLRB) elections.

Admittedly, differentially counteracting trends both between sectors and between specific industries are impossible to equate. However, the total evidence seems to confirm that the UAW has been substantially more successful in attracting white-collar members than has been typically true of the other industrial unions in the last five years.

I am convinced, on the basis of my own investigations before

---

[19] U.S. Bureau of Labor Statistics, *Directory of Labor Unions, 1969*, p. 97. The 1968 figure was reaffirmed by a union representative in my interviews in 1971.

[20] Technical-Office-Professional Department report cited in *White-Collar Report*, no. 584, May 16, 1968, p. A-7.

[21] See Cohany, "Trends and Changes in Union Membership," pp. 511–512.

[22] Data are from the U.S. Bureau of Labor Statistics, *Directory of National and International Labor Unions in the United States, 1967*, cited in *White-Collar Report*, no. 606, October 17, 1968, pp. B-4 to B-8.

1963 and in 1967–68, that a merely passive continuation of past UAW efforts in this area would *not* have permitted the Union to show the white-collar gains which it has recently achieved. Although the external organizing climate is much improved over that of the late 1950's, this does not adequately explain the sharp differential improvement in UAW white-collar performance.

Solving the White-Collar Problem

Both statistical evidence and interview materials confirm significant reversal of the UAW's fortunes in the white-collar field since 1961. In the following pages I shall attempt to record and explain the processes that have resulted in one industrial union's increasing success in meeting the white-collar thrust of today's economy. But it should be clear from the limited absolute magnitude of the membership and organizing statistics cited above that much remains to be accomplished before one can state that the UAW has entirely "solved" the white-collar problem.

This qualification should not obscure the significance of the substantial progress that the Union has made in this area. From the experience of the UAW and other unions the all-important *direction* of required institutional change is now becoming increasingly clear. For those who remember the general pessimism, confusion, and stalemate that existed concerning this problem in the late 1950's, the gains seem truly amazing.

The Significance of the UAW's Efforts

The immediate relevance of the Autoworkers' white-collar effort to the general problem of union growth should be recognized. The UAW has affirmatively answered the question whether white-collar workers can be successfully organized by an industrial union in today's economy. This accomplishment demonstrates that one institutional form which white-collar unionism will be able to take in the future is that of an industrial unit— one that is closely related to existing unionism among an industry's blue-collar production workers. Viable, vital white-collar unionism is thus entirely practical on an industrial basis.

The UAW experience is adaptable to the requirements of other unions in the industrial bloc of the labor movement, given intelligent experimentation and the willingness to commit resources to the problem. It is apparent, however, that each union must fashion its own special version of those changes in accord with its unique situation and industry. By extrapolation, it is clear that such a capability has far-reaching implications for the continued influence of industrial union leadership within the American labor movement.

It also follows that management in manufacturing will be increasingly faced with the prospect of collective bargaining among its white-collar employees, just as nonmanufacturing management and administrative officials elsewhere in the economy are now encountering white-collar unionism for the first time.

Social and Theoretical Importance

From a theoretical standpoint at least two important and broadly encompassing social considerations can be related to the UAW experience: representation and bureaucratization.

The issue of adequate economic and social representation of the growing white-collar group in our society is well stated by Adolf Sturmthal:

> The drive toward what the French call the *économie concertée* —a society based upon consensus among the main social forces —may contribute to the need for organization of groups which in the past were reluctant to organize. For, in practice, consensus is agreement among organizations rather than individuals and the *économie concertée* rests upon consultation and compromises among spokesmen of organized groups. Power relationships thus underlie consensus and concert.[23]

Social scientists have repeatedly emphasized the growing bureaucratization of American society in the post–World War II

[23] Sturmthal, ed., *White-Collar Trade Unions*, p. vi.

period. It thus becomes of vital social concern whether a key American institution such as a 1.5 million-member union can successfully innovate in response to changes in its environment as fundamental as those posed by the shift in the characteristics of the labor force examined above.[24]

In 1960 the UAW and other unions seemed excellent examples of bureaucratic rigidity and internal political stalemate. They paralyzed action and prejudiced the long-term survival and continuing influence of unions in the economy.

By 1968 UAW performance offered a basis for qualified optimism in the white-collar area. Here was an important demonstration of institutional flexibility. Thus, to the extent that this huge union has been able to successfully adapt its constitutional structure, its leadership's attitudes and views, and its organizing and bargaining methods to new labor force characteristics, there can be a more hopeful interpretation of the future of industrial society itself.

Sturmthal identifies the broad social significance of these trends:

> The progress of industrialization . . . gradually undermines the division of society that has been inherited from the past. The traditional class structure related to status does not fit the requirements of an industrial society. . . . [Group distinctions] express the value system of the industrial society, a value system intimately related to achievement, market valuations, and the functions performed rather than status. This evolving change . . . is in essence what is called the "process of democratization" characteristic of the rise of the industrial society.[25]

[24] See Marvin Friedman, "The Changing Profile of the Labor Force," *AFL-CIO American Federationist,* July, 1967, pp. 7–14, for a broad summary of these changing characteristics as seen by a union representative.

[25] Sturmthal, "White-Collar Unions—A Comparative Essay," in Sturmthal, ed., *White-Collar Trade Unions,* p. 387.

White-Collar Workers: "A Different Breed of Cat"

2

One of the consistent mistakes of blue-collar-based unions in white-collar organizing has been their tendency to deny the existence or importance of the unique characteristics of white-collar workers.

In part this denial has probably been a reflection of a tradition of ill feeling between the office and the shop. White-collar workers often looked down on the shop and on the shopworkers' organization, the union. There was—and is—an obstacle, though often exaggerated, in the "white-collar snob."

Perhaps in reaction, the shopworker developed his own prejudices about white-collar workers, who may be seen as "soft" and "cozied up" to "the Boss." As Whiting Williams has observed, in many ways the shop has been a male society. The office milieu has had historically more of the characteristics of a female society.[1] In broader terms this concept may also be useful in explaining certain differences in the value systems of the working class and the middle class.[2]

Generally we may say that the industrial union must meet the problem of organizing across a class barrier, though this barrier

[1] Whiting Williams, "Guarding the Goodwill of White-Collar Workers," *Factory Management and Maintenance,* December, 1944, pp. 117–118.

[2] Note S. M. Miller's useful distinction between the terms "lower class" and "the working class" in "The New Working Class," in Arthur B. Shostak and William Gomberg, eds., *The Blue-Collar World: Studies of the American Worker* (Englewood Cliffs, N.J.: Prentice-Hall, 1964), pp. 2–8.

is quite amorphous in the United States.[3] If successful, it must subsequently provide structurally, educationally, and programmatically for the most harmonious cooperation between these disparate groups within a single organization. That this is a practical possibility is demonstrated by the experience of the UAW over the past thirty years.

A Problem in Images

A useful way to analyze the organizing problem of unions in relating to white-collar workers is by considering four dimensions: the self-image of white-collar workers; their perceived image of the union; the specific pressures in the unique organizing situation; and the resultant acceptance or rejection of the union as a personal option of choice by a majority of the group.

The white-collar worker's image of himself—what he is, what he wants to be—is balanced against his perception of the union's image. If the organizing situation is sufficiently intense, the images become compatible. They are congruent enough for the white-collar worker to opt for the union.

The self-image tends to be stable in the short run. The image of the union is also quite stable. However, the white-collar worker's awareness of his true position and his perception of the union may be at least marginally modified by the organizer's projection of the union alternative; thus the key importance of appropriate language, organizing literature, and manner for the organizer. These represent the union specifically and concretely to the potential member. The intensity of the pressures operating in the particular organizing situation are the resources subject to exploitation by both the organizer and his management opposition. The election vote measures the result of the contending forces.

In the longer run the larger context of trends in the economy

---

[3] Albert Blum mentions the element of class identification as related to management. See *Management and the White-Collar Union* (New York: American Management Association, 1964), pp. 49–52.

may operate to enhance or diminish the self-image of the white-collar worker. An example here is the oft-cited movement toward mechanization and routinization of office-clerical and, eventually, technical tasks. Economic and social changes and the union's conscious attempt to take thought of its own institutional characteristics and to consciously modify its behavior can increase the acceptability of the union image as perceived by unorganized workers. For example, does the union appear cognizant of white-collar identity, differing needs, and special preferences? Does it appear responsible in its use of power, yet militant enough to offer a practical possibility of improving the white-collar worker's position? Is the union leadership honest, alert, responsive, socially aware, and capable of speaking white-collar language? These characteristics might all be summed up as relevant to the white-collar worker's concern for respectability.

There is thus an important possibility of developing a reinforcing relationship between the union's internal program for its white-collar members and increasing external organizing success.

What Is a White-Collar Worker?

Although most people have a roughly workable understanding of the term "white-collar worker," a definition may be desirable here. In addition to the Department of Labor usage mentioned above, Carol Barry has summarized the common characteristics of white-collar occupations. These jobs lack any special work clothes requirement—hence the white collar. The work is usually performed in an office rather than in the factory itself. The effort required is largely mental. Formal education is stressed. There were once favorable pay differentials and superior fringe benefits, including paid vacation, holidays, and sick leaves. A greater degree of job security is assumed. Payment is by salary rather than by hourly wages.[4]

Needless to say, the definition above represents a cluster of

[4] Carol Barry, "Special Labor Force Report," *Monthly Labor Review*, January, 1961, pp. 11–18.

characteristics, one or more of which may be absent in the case of any specific worker or occupation.

From a practical standpoint, attention here must focus primarily upon the clerical and technical workers in industry. To date, industrial unions have had little success in the higher reaches of the white-collar spectrum. The professional worker is clearly resistant to inclusion in industry units. As a case in point, the UAW's entire white-collar professional membership was probably accurately measured by its initial per capita payment of 1,000 to the professional group of the AFL-CIO—the Council of Scientific, Professional, and Cultural Employees.[5]

Long-run improvement in the industrial unions' appeal to professional employees is not impossible, but this may come only after initial self-organization by professionals. If so, union gains will then be contingent upon the typical failure of professional units to coalesce into a self-supporting association with adequate bargaining skills and power.

Office-Clerical Workers

Most upper-class people derive their images of the white-collar people largely from stereotypes of the "clerk."
—C. Wright Mills[6]

Historically, the white-collar clerical worker seems to have developed as an agent or representative of the enterpriser. He was thus entrusted with semi-entrepreneurial functions. His original close association with the enterpriser may have persisted as a feeling of being a part of management long after increased scale and the rationalization of production destroyed the functional basis for such a relationship.[7]

[5] Interview data by author.
[6] C. Wright Mills, "The Middle Classes in Middle-Sized Cities," *American Sociological Review*, December, 1946, p. 527.
[7] See Arne H. Nilstein, "White-Collar Unionism in Sweden," in Adolf Sturmthal, ed., *White-Collar Trade Unions* (Urbana: University of Illinois Press, 1966), p. 263. This is Fritz Croner's conclusion. See his "Salaried Employees in Modern Society," *International Labour Review*, February, 1954, p. 109.

In any event, it seems clear that the white-collar worker's reluctance to unionize must be explained in more than economic terms. Social and psychological factors, as so usefully emphasized by sociologist C. Wright Mills, are of paramount importance in explaining the seeming economic irrationality of the group.[8] Only now, long after the extensive organization of blue-collar craft and industrial workers, are we beginning to see the spread of unionization among Mills's "new middle class" of captive professionals, technicians, and clerks as they slowly become aware of their differentiation from the "old middle class" of businessmen and free professionals.

White-collar workers' characteristics identified in the literature appear sufficiently typical to give a useful portrait of the clerical group. Technicians are significantly different and thus will be considered separately.

The Clerk

A composite portrait of the clerical white-collar worker would include a relatively strong concern for status advancement, a view of work as a career, high valuation of formal education, and a middle-class pattern of home and leisure activities and interests.[9] He identifies strongly with concepts of individualism and has an ability to imagine himself as part of management—if not now, then in the indefinite future.[10]

The clerical worker tends to be clannish in the industrial work situation; he distinguishes himself from factory workers by better grammar and by a more restrained and self-conscious use of profanity. He also places a great value upon keeping clean while at work, and he is attached to the set of work conditions which supports this and other associated aspects of his self-image. There

[8] C. Wright Mills, *White Collar: The American Middle Classes* (New York: Oxford University Press, 1951).

[9] See, for example, Herman J. Loether, "The Meaning of Work and Adjustment to Retirement," in Shostak and Gomberg, *Blue-Collar World*, pp. 517–525.

[10] Robert K. Burns, "Unionization of the White-Collar Worker," *Personnel Series No. 110* (New York: American Management Association, 1947), pp. 3–16.

is an important element of truth in George Strauss's remark, "To them unions are dirty, noisy, and lower class—as well as contrary to their Horatio Alger dream of working up from office boy to president."[11]

In sum, the industrial union seeking entrance to the office comes into contact with people "whose interests and conceptions of themselves are different from those of the typical factory worker"—people with a persistent desire to maintain a separate identity. It is all too easy for the union to make the error of seeking to impose its own image of the white-collar worker upon this group, rather than seeking to discover and work with the white-collar worker's own self-image.[12]

Let us look next at a group of white-collar workers with certain special characteristics: the technicians.

The New Mechanics

The ramifying complexity of modern technology has called into being a modern version of the traditional mechanic—a new mechanic with heightened social aspirations, increased dependence upon formal education or training, and wearing the white-collar badge.

Although increasingly numerous in industry, the technicians have received relatively little systematic study. Most of the few investigations of this group have been directed toward those types of technicians who support scientists and engineers in research and scientific activities, rather than toward those (such as in this discussion) who are associated with product design and process engineering.

In industry the technicians are basically "men in the middle" between the degree engineers and the highly skilled craft work-

[11] George Strauss, "White-Collar Unions Are Different!" *Harvard Business Review,* September–October, 1954, pp. 73–82.

[12] Benjamin Solomon, "The Problems and Areas of Union Expansion in the White Collar Sector," *Proceedings of Ninth Annual Meeting* (Madison, Wis.: Industrial Relations Research Association, 1957), pp. 238–243. He credits John W. McCollum of the Union Research and Education Project, University of Chicago, with this concept.

ers. William Evan points out, "The hallmark of the technician, especially at the higher levels, is his unique blend of some professional knowledge and manual or instrumental skill."[13] The technician in industry is somewhat easier to organize than the professional worker. However, he presents a special problem because his loyalty and aspirations are directed toward the normally anti-union professional engineers. He works closely with these engineers and takes them as a reference group.[14] Yet he is usually rebuffed in his attempt to make common cause with the engineers in forming collective bargaining units.

A typical pattern is that found in a study of automobile draftsmen in the Detroit area. Only sixteen of sixty-nine such technicians expressed pro-union sympathies. Significantly, their largely negative view of unionism seemed to reflect the entire life situation and background of the draftsmen.[15]

Engineers in the UAW

Despite the technician's anti-union disposition, he does—if given sufficient provocation—sometimes choose to become a union member. For example, nearly 4,000 of this group at the Chrysler Corporation have elected UAW representation.

Here it is important to note that most so-called engineering workers in the automobile industry are *not* professional engineers with degrees from institutions of advanced collegiate training.[16] Although there are some degree-holding engineers in the industry, their numbers appear relatively insignificant. On the other

[13] William H. Evan, "On the Margin—The Engineering Technician," in Peter L. Berger, ed., *The Human Shape of Work* (New York: Macmillan, 1964), pp. 85, 89.

[14] Paul K. Hatt and C. C. North rate clerical workers 68.2, trained machinists 73, public school teachers 78, and professional and semi-professional workers 80.6 in their "Prestige Ratings of Occupations," in Sigmund Nosow and William Form, *Man, Work, and Society* (New York: Basic Books, 1962), pp. 277–283.

[15] See Kay H. Smith, "A Psychological Inquiry into Attitudes of Industrial Draftsmen toward Unionism," (Ph.D. dissertation, Wayne State University, 1961), pp. 158, 170.

[16] Nelson N. Foote, "The Professionalization of Labor in Detroit," *American Journal of Sociology*, January, 1953, pp. 371–380.

hand, engineering technicians perform a multitude of highly skilled tasks for the auto companies. For instance, "Schedule A" of the contract between the Chrysler Corporation and the UAW covers "engineering" employees. It specifies such jobs as the following: tool, die, and fixture engineers; process engineers; plant layout engineers; and "engineering employees." The much more frequent type of classification is clearly technical: body detailer, chassis drafting detailer, clay modeler, follow-up man, tool trouble man, designer, draftsman, tool and die designer.[17]

Profile of an Automobile Engineer

An interesting composite of characteristics emerge from interviews with these employees. One of their most outstanding traits is an intense consciousness of the importance of the job itself. They approach the completely "job-oriented" view and appear to be even more career-conscious than the typical office-clerical worker. If the engineering-technical worker is not always personally creative, he is at least very close to the creative processes in the industry. Thus he is strongly aware of the necessity of making way for exceptional individual talent.

The engineering-technical worker tends to be mobile within the industry. This is particularly facilitated by the concentration of automotive design activity in the Detroit area. He has probably gained his skill and improved his economic position by moving upward through a series of job-shop positions. Frequently he has moved laterally between the engineering departments of at least two of the Big Three.

He values education highly, not only in his trade but in general. He is frequently taking, or has recently taken, night school courses on his own initiative.

His strategic position in the automobile industry during and since World War II has, until very recently, made him largely immune to the layoffs periodically experienced by shopworkers —layoffs which occasionally reach the ranks of the industry's

[17] See *Agreement between Chrysler Corporation and the UAW: Engineering,* November 2, 1961, pp. 93–100.

office-clerical employees. Thus the automotive engineer-technician has been little concerned with the threat of unemployment. He is firmly convinced that individual bargaining and the local area mobility which he possesses are adequate to protect his personal economic interests.

As a technician he frequently looks upon the shop union as an irritation. It is an obstacle in his daily routine as he moves between drawing board and plant floor. He is quickly called to account by the shop union when he oversteps job classification lines at the boundary of the shop contract. (This may happen easily during the course of his trouble-shooting activities or in the construction of experimental models.) Thus the shop union's ever present concern with protecting "its" jobs against encroachment often strikes him as more unrealistic and costly to the company than it may appear to the office worker.

White-Collar Attitudes in the Auto Industry

The substantial accomplishment of the UAW in its white-collar organizing activities deserves to be measured against the initially negative attitudes of eligible employees in the auto industry.

In the preceding discussion I have looked generally at typical white-collar characteristics, the self-image of these workers, and implications for their view of the union. Now it is desirable to introduce more specifically the reactions of white-collar automobile industry employees as revealed in interviews during the 1959–63 period.[18]

The organizing obstacle presented by these attitudes is significantly magnified by management's manipulation of them to forestall unionization. Thus thoroughgoing attitude studies seem to offer a fundamental tool for any industrial union contemplating expansion in the white-collar field.

Here the attitude materials are presented as part of the historical background which will be considered from several other

---

[18] For further details on interview methods, see Carl Dean Snyder, "Industrial Unions Can Lose the Battle for the White-Collar Worker: The UAW as a Case in Point" (D.S.Sc. dissertation, Syracuse University, 1964).

vantage points in future chapters. Although some shifts in attitudes occur over time, much of this interview material still seems very representative of current white-collar views. It thus delineates the typical obstacles normally faced by the white-collar organizer.

Interview Methods

A total of over one hundred interviews varying from one to three hours in length were conducted among white-collar workers in the Detroit-area auto industry from 1959 to 1963. Some stratification was used to insure representation of employees from each of the major auto firms, from supplier companies, and to cut across the clerical and technical occupational categories.

It is important to note that multiple responses were received on most items. Consequently, percentage calculations throughout the discussion are based on the number of responses compared to the number of respondents to each individual item— *not* upon the number of persons interviewed in each portion of the sample. Thus instances in which percentages total more than 100 are frequent in the tables and discussions that follow.[19]

For present purposes it appears unnecessarily awkward to continually specify *N* for each item. The reader can assume that this will be between eighteen and twenty-five for each group. Specific exceptions are noted. The author's basic technical study provides this information in detail for readers who wish to check further on any individual item.

Self-Image: Group Difference

A fundamental part of the white-collar worker's self-image is that his group has a distinctive identity. Thus 73 percent of unorganized white-collar workers in the sample responded that

---

[19] See especially Ch. 2, "Additive Multiple Answers," in Hans Zeisel, *Say It with Figures* (New York: Harper and Brothers, 1947), pp. 21–38. The discussion of the method of calculation used in the present study and the form used in tabular presentations here are found on pp. 22–25.

there were "important differences" between themselves and shop-workers as groups. The nature of these differences was concentrated in four areas: the "coarseness" of the behavior and language of shopworkers, their lower social class, the higher education of white-collar workers, and, less strongly, the identification of white-collar workers with management.

Insight concerning the white-collar worker's self-image is also to be found in his reasons for choosing white-collar work. Prominent mention was given to (in order) the possibility of advancement, the nature of the work itself (variety, challenge, interest), working conditions (cleanliness, dress, etc.), greater job security than in the shop, and the urging of parents who hoped their children would avoid factory work.

Only 17 percent of the unorganized white-collar group felt that they had entered this type of work by "pure accident." This implies a significant commitment to their particular occupational grouping stemming from conscious personal choice.

In a related question, seeking to identify those characteristics of white-collar jobs which were most liked, answers indicated that 35 percent of the group valued the prestige involved in the position and 17 percent specifically included "contact with management" and "better people."

The possible repercussions of the spreading work rationalization process in white-collar occupations can be identified in this group's observation that what most white-collar workers "liked least" was monotony on the job and the pressure of deadlines in work scheduling. Significantly, nearly 40 percent stated that they had personally experienced increased work pressure during the preceding five to ten years.

The strong mobility striving of the unorganized white-collar group was a marked characteristic: 87 percent aspired to a higher position. Some measure of this commitment is the fact that eighteen of the twenty-three respondents on this item had, at some time, secured specialized training beyond their general academic preparation. This included technical courses, night school, business college work, company-sponsored programs, and other activities.

The job orientation of this group was strongly positive. Sixty-one percent rated their jobs as "very important" to the success of their company. Another 30 percent saw these jobs as "fairly important." It seems probable that this orientation is an important contributing factor to the strong identification of these workers with management interests. When asked, "In general, do you feel that whatever is in the best interests of your employer is also usually best for you?" 91 percent of respondents answered affirmatively.

The Unorganized White-Collar Worker's Perception of Unions

The image of unions which white-collar workers perceive has often been assumed to be inherently incompatible with their self-image. But, in reality, this union image is a mixed one. Unions have assets as well as liabilities in the minds of white-collar employees—a fact which is indispensable in explaining those instances in which union membership becomes acceptable, given favoring circumstances in the job situation.

Reversing the usual emphasis, let us look first at the positive aspects of the union image. Interviews made clear that 78 percent of respondents thought that unions, as a whole, had been responsible for more good than bad in American life. Only 9 percent felt that unions were overall negative influences in American life. Thirteen percent took an intermediate position.

A positive evaluation of unions appeared also in the opinion of 86 percent of the group that unions were necessary for hourly rated production workers. An additional 5 percent held them to be sometimes necessary.

In an attempt to discover the symbolic associations of the term "union" in the minds of white-collar workers, interviewees were asked to name "the first thing that comes to mind" when thinking of unions. Thirty-eight percent of respondents mentioned seniority and job protection while 19 percent said strikes. Thirteen percent named better working conditions, while a like number mentioned violence, corruption, or racketeering as characteristic of unions. Six percent mentioned wage increases. Interestingly, in view of the conservatism frequently imputed to white-collar workers, only 6 percent identified radicalism as a union characteristic.

An important special asset of the UAW with white-collar workers in the Detroit area was that it appeared as a unique union—not as simply a stereotype. Thus almost 40 percent of the randomly selected sample of unorganized white-collar workers held that the UAW was better than other unions, while only 6 percent thought it might be worse than other unions.

In this same direction it was significant that the group also differentiated sharply between types of labor leaders. Seventy percent of the group indicated that they held high esteem for some particular labor leader.

A key element in the projection of any individual union's image is the personality and character of its leadership. The success of the UAW in the white-collar field is certainly related to the finding that 81 percent of those with high esteem for a labor leader identified this person as Walter Reuther, president of the UAW.

Union Weaknesses

The negative features in the unorganized white-collar worker's perceived union image were highlighted in the responses included in Table 2–1.

TABLE 2–1. CHANGES IN UNION BEHAVIOR DESIRED
BY UNORGANIZED WHITE-COLLAR WORKERS

Question: Are there any particular changes you would like to see in the way unions are run and in the way they act?

Unions should be less militant	42%
Unions should be more democratic in internal affairs	37
Less corruption within unions is desirable	26
Unions should have better leadership	26
Unions should do less in politics	11
Unions should issue less propaganda	5
Other (miscellaneous)	16

Personal responses to these union characteristics were reflected in answers to a question concerning the effect of union membership upon the prestige of white-collar workers. Fifty-nine percent held that white-collar workers saw union membership as reducing their prestige.

One oft-cited handicap of the union in appealing to white-collar workers is its political activity. This is alleged to be disturbing to the more conservative employees in this group. In spite of many years of repeated efforts by political opponents and conservative journalists to establish the UAW as "radical" or "Communistic," interviews consistently demonstrated that the political dimension was a vastly overrated deterrent. Although 43 percent of the unorganized group believed that unions should not work toward the election of candidates to public office, most agreed that this issue was not sufficiently important to adversely affect a representation election.

From interview results it appears that a considerable portion of the white-collar workers in a given industry can be reached through the shop union's newspaper. Seventy-eight percent of the respondents in the unorganized group had, at some time, read union newspapers. Seventy-two percent of respondents had read such a source several times, and 28 percent had read it often. Fifty-two percent had watched a union-sponsored television program; 43 percent voluntarily mentioned hearing the local UAW-presented radio program.

To counter the usual union stereotypes played upon in the public press, it appears that the union must rely primarily upon its own channels and upon personal contacts.

Ineffective Publications

However, respondents' reactions to such union communications indicated the existence of a significant need for improvement. Only 6 percent of the unorganized white-collar group were favorable to union publications. Television and radio efforts were somewhat better received, with 33 percent of the group giving a favorable reaction.

A final confirmation of the white-collar worker's self-image and its implications for union organization can be seen in the desire of white-collar workers for a form of organization which sharply differentiates between themselves and shopworkers. Although white-collar workers will, and do, join industrial unions, they have a strong initial preference for an entirely white-collar union.

If a union such as the Office and Professional Employees International Union had sufficient resources to actively compete with the industrial unions in areas of disputed jurisdiction, it seems likely that it could attract a large share of the unorganized group in industry. Thus it is worth noting that just over 60 percent of the unorganized group had a strong preference for an entirely office and professional workers' union rather than the UAW. Another 20 percent had at least a mild preference for that alternative.

The persistence of this preference is reflected in the attitude of two independent organizing groups at the Ford Motor Company in 1971. Neither was interested in UAW affiliation because the union was seen as dominated by its production and maintenance members.[20]

From this it seems clear that there is an imperative requirement for the industrial union to provide the maximum possible degree of autonomy for the white-collar segment. This will help to attract new white-collar members, as well as serving to meet the preferences of its already acquired white-collar membership.

The Union Option

The payoff question in analyzing white-collar unionization is whether or not the white-collar worker will choose union membership when the opportunity arises.

There is little doubt that most white-collar workers have not yet been explicitly challenged to make this decision. Total union organizing efforts in the white-collar field have been relatively minuscule and tentative.

[20] See *White-Collar Report,* no. 731, March 12, 1971, p. A-2.

However, the widespread reluctance of white-collar workers to accept unionization has been indirectly measured both by specific studies and by the overall trend of results in those organizing attempts which have been made. The important exceptions to this reluctance which are now appearing—teachers, nurses, and public employees—are noteworthy because they are still atypical.

The lack of fit between the white-collar worker's self-image and his perceived image of unions was summed up in two ways in interviews. While strongly agreeing that unions were necessary for production workers, only 14 percent of the unorganized white-collar workers interviewed thought that unions were necessary for white-collar workers. An additional 5 percent thought them sometimes necessary. On the other hand, these workers did not completely reject unionization as an alternative: 50 percent stated that they would join under certain circumstances. Three types of such circumstances were most frequently identified; these included the arbitrary use of authority by management, the occurrence of an organizing trend among white-collar workers, and increased pressure on the job. These two latter developments seem to have an increasing probability in the long run, as will appear in more detail in the final chapter.

Management's Resistance

The characteristic attitudes of unorganized white-collar workers are the major cause of limited unionization among this group. However, an important supplement to this inherent white-collar reluctance is the disapproving, anti-union attitude of management toward white-collar organization and the specific policies which implement this attitude.[21]

[21] Among the most thorough early treatments of white-collar unionization as a problem for management are the publications of the National Association of Manufacturers. See, for example, *Satisfying the Salaried Employee* (New York: Industrial Relations Division, National Association of Manufacturers, April, 1957), pp. 8–16, and *A Report to Management on Unionization of Salaried Employees* (New York: Industrial Relations Division, National Association of Manufacturers, October, 1958), pp. 5–6.

Several factors are typically involved in management's resistance to white-collar unionization. First, there is a psychological element. Management is concerned over the "loyalty" of its white-collar workers. This is perhaps partly due to vanity. But more important, management seems to fear that a close supporter and ally may go over to the "enemy." Second, there is the possible loss of flexibility of operation. Unions are seen as a threat to management's traditional freedom to manage the office efficiently (or, the union charges, with management's historical caprice and arbitrariness). Third, there is the prospect of higher costs: costs arising from classification restrictions on the movement of employees between jobs, increased salary and benefit costs, and representation costs. Fourth, in the case of professional and technical employees, management fears that the creativity of this group might be adversely affected by the impact of union seniority policies. Thus the competitive survival of the company is felt to be imperiled by unionism.

Management's View of White-Collar Workers

In general, the view of the white-collar worker obtained in interviews with twenty-one members of automobile management agreed quite well with the unorganized white-collar worker's view of himself. Management generally has a higher regard for the white-collar employee and his characteristics than it does for the blue-collar worker. Management tends to see him as being both different from and, in terms of management's value system, superior to the shopworker.

Thus there seems to be no sizable "value gap" between management and the white-collar group such as tends to be true of management and the blue-collar group.[22] Not only does this sharing of common values operate reciprocally; it probably

[22] Roethlisberger and Dickson in their famous study designated two contrasting systems of ideas and beliefs which reflect these differing values: a "logic of cost and efficiency" and an often contrasting "logic of sentiments." See F. J. Roethlisberger and William J. Dickson, *Management and the Worker* (Cambridge: Harvard University Press, 1942), pp. 563–565.

moderates the interpersonal impact of the entire superior-subordinate authority relationship as well.

In exploring the question of white-collar "difference" only 12 percent of the management interviewees believed that these differences were insignificant and that blue- and white-collar workers were "all alike."

Management representatives strongly emphasized the characteristics which implied differing social class (such as language patterns and educational level), the white-collar worker's interest in prestige and advancement, nearness to management, and the lesser emotionality (and militance!) of white-collar workers as compared to blue-collar employees.

Opposition to Unionization

Management in the automobile industry has consistently expressed its conviction that white-collar workers have no need for union representation.[23] In the interviews with management representatives only 7 percent stated that their companies accepted unionization for the office and technical personnel. Seventy-three percent either strongly opposed such unionization or preferred freedom from unionization. However, 20 percent stated that their company had no definite policy in this regard.

A great deal of attention has been given by management and associated organizations to forestalling white-collar unionization. So far this has been accomplished by an extensive consideration of the nature of the white-collar worker. From this follows a systematic attempt to meet his needs by tailoring a comprehensive personnel program that will minimize the white-collar employee's interest in "outside" representation.

Writing for the American Management Association, Albert Blum identifies the elements of such a program to include good salaries, excellent fringe benefits, channels for upward and down-

[23] For example, in relation to the UAW's 1965 organizing drive, Henry Ford II was quoted as saying, "I don't think they're going to be able to organize us because our policies are good and we think our relations with salaried employees are excellent." See *White-Collar Report,* no. 459, December 23, 1965, p. A-1.

ward communication, the settlement of grievances, a recognition of individual differences, superior supervision, different treatment to foster the continued identification of white-collar employees with management, job security, upward mobility, and special privileges.[24]

Interviews with management representatives in the auto industry confirmed that the most frequent company response to the threat of white-collar unionization was a comprehensive personnel program which strongly emphasized an attractive salary and benefit program. In autos the latter has meant a systematic "tandem" granting of improvements following (or sometimes slightly exceeding) the pattern of shop-negotiated settlements. Management also mentioned the use of individual talks with employees, a voluntary observation of seniority as (at least) an important factor in promotion and layoff, and special attention to white-collar employees, as well as extra supervision.

Unmentioned but significant were the special campaigns by management to offset specific union organizing efforts. Informal comments to the author from sources (both management and union) outside the companies directly concerned maintained that the carrying out of such "anti-white-collar unionism" programs at General Motors and Ford have involved both sizable staffs and substantial financial commitments.

[24] Blum, *Management and the White-Collar Union,* pp. 11–12. He cites a sound personnel program as "the most important means of suppressing the appeal of unionism for their white-collar people" (p. 14).

White Collarites—
A Dubious Blessing

3

With this introduction to the nature of the white-collar worker and the problem which this nature presents to the industrial union, we can now usefully examine the historical experience of the UAW in the white-collar field.

In a theoretical sense we are tracing the adaptation of an institution (a "bureaucracy") and its ideology to changing circumstances in its environment during a thirty-year period. From this we will conclude that an industrial union, if it is to be successful in white-collar organizing, must make changes in structure, ideology, and internal processes—as well as in leadership, staff, and member attitudes and relationships. These modifications are necessary to meet the needs and expectations of a new clientele.

In general, the UAW moved from an early rejection and dismissal of possible white-collar organization to an indifferent acceptance of such workers. This was accompanied by an ideological emphasis upon homogeneity and integration in industrial units. Ultimately an emerging explicit recognition of group differences leads to structural changes adequate to meet the requirements of white-collar workers. This process has been aided in certain ways by the somewhat parallel skilled trades challenge to the industrial union concept.

During these years the white-collar membership of the UAW was increasing and becoming aware of its problems as a group within the industrial union framework. It eventually acquired sufficient political skill to attain recognition, attention, and a more nearly adequate response from the top leadership of the Union.

Three Historical Strands

From a consideration of the white-collar activities of the UAW since the late 1930's one can identify three themes with marked continuity. One was the autonomous organizing efforts of automobile industry technicians, the Society of Designing Engineers (SDE).

The Society originated in the same social ferment of the middle 1930's that gave rise to the Congress of Industrial Organizations (CIO) itself. At Chrysler this organization became the nucleus for the incorporation of technicians into the UAW. At General Motors the initial enthusiasm and success of the SDE was ultimately contained and obliterated within the corporation. At Ford blue-collar expediency in bargaining away white-collar organizing rights created extensive resentment among that company's technicians. Even today this continues to be a major liability of the UAW with this group of employees. Incidentally, it is also a persistent thorn in the side of Ford management, in the form of festering problems at Dearborn Engineering. Among supplier firms in the industry technical units deriving from the SDE endure to the present day as parts of UAW local unions.

A second theme was the explicit exclusion of white-collar workers—most pronounced at Ford, but important elsewhere in the Union as well. The third strand is the theme of organizing "along the corporate chain" as developed most extensively at the Chrysler Corporation, particularly among the office-clerical groups.

The Society of Designing Engineers

From available information it appears that effective white-collar unionization in the automobile industry occurred earliest among the technical workers. The independent Society of Designing

Engineers was formed in December, 1932, to improve the employment status of mechanical engineers, draftsmen, and designers.[1] The earliest evidence of office-worker organization was at Kelsey-Hayes in 1937. The SDE was engaged in widespread organizing activity in the 1935–38 period at a level not reached in the automobile clerical worker area until 1941.

In one of the earliest cases brought before the National Labor Relations Board, the Society filed a petition for an investigation and certification of representation on October 22, 1935. "The petition stated that the Union represented 460 of the 700 designing engineers employed by the Chrysler Corporation. . . ."[2]

Extent of SDE Activity

By February, 1936, the membership of the Society of Designing Engineers was approximately 2,300, according to the NLRB case cited above.[3] Another source reported a membership of 3,000 at about the same time.[4]

In a 1936 interview it was stated: "Practically all the body draftsmen in the industry are organized in the SDA [*sic*]. VH says there are only 600 body draftsmen in the whole USA. Extent of org. is indicated by fact that at Briggs all but six of the 150 draftsmen and engineering specialists are members. Tool and die designers are also strong in SDA."[5] The Briggs SDE engineering unit eventually joined UAW-CIO Local 212 in October, 1943.

By 1938 the Society may have been feeling the effects of its exposed position. A UAW Publicity Bureau news release stated that the SDE then claimed only 1,500 members, as compared to the CIO's Federation of Architects, Engineers, Chemists, and

---

[1] See "In the Matter of Chrysler Corporation and Society of Designing Engineers," Case no. R-16, decided February 14, 1936, 1 *NLRB* 164. Reported in *Labor Relations Reference Manual,* 1937, p. 364.

[2] *Ibid.*

[3] *Ibid.*, p. 366.

[4] See "Interview with VH on Society of Designing Engineers," in "Society of Designing Engineers—Organization and Administration," Brown Collection, Archives, Wayne State University Library.

[5] *Ibid.*

Technicians' 10,000. There were then SDE chapters in Detroit, Pontiac, Flint, Lansing, Jackson, Toledo, South Bend, Cleveland, Kenosha ". . . and other cities."[6] In a referendum the SDE voted to affiliate with FAECT. However, it explicitly retained its autonomous position within the larger organization.

In June, 1938, the Detroit chapter's *News Flash* announced that "Under the Briggs Contract, the Detroit Chapter of the SDE (now Chapter #201 of the FAECT) is the recognized bargaining agency." As confirmation of the importance of the event, the publication noted comments by the *Wall Street Journal* and *Business Week*.[7]

The SDE at General Motors and Ford

In view of the UAW's continuing inability to gain significant entry to the white-collar occupations at both Ford and General Motors, SDE progress at both of these companies in the early 1940's now appears phenomenal. The Society's *News Flash* for July 2, 1941, carried the announcement that "S.D.E.— F.A.E.C.T. Makes Clean Sweep in General Motors Elections." The item went on to state, ". . . last week, three G. M. Units cast overwhelming votes in favor of the SDE as sole collective bargaining agent in N.L.R.B. elections, for the draftsmen, designers, and allied employees (engineering record clerks, blueprint clerks, etc.) in the Styling, Cadillac and Ternstedt plants."[8] The results of the elections showed the SDE gaining 70 percent of the vote in "Styling," 92 percent in the Cadillac unit, and 98 percent in the Ternstedt plant.

On another page a brief note claimed that "Majority of Ford Technical Staff is Enrolled by S.D.E." The union publication held that a total of 800 members had been enrolled during the preceding month.[9]

[6] UAW Publicity Bureau, "News Release," February 7, 1938, Brown Collection.

[7] "News Flash," Organizing Committee of Detroit Chapter 201, Society of Designing Engineers, June 8, 1938, p. 1, Brown Collection.

[8] "News Flash," Society of Designing Engineers, FAECT-CIO, July 2, 1941, p. 1, Brown Collection.

[9] *Ibid.*, p. 2.

Two weeks later the same publication indicated that the SDE's field representative had succeeded in signing up "a large majority" of the approximately one hundred draftsmen and designers at Ex-Cell-O Corporation.[10]

The SDE Changes Affiliation

After a brief period of affiliation with the FAECT, in October, 1942, the Society petitioned the national CIO for permission to transfer all of its membership to the UAW-CIO. Following a joint election among the members concerned in Detroit, Flint, and Toledo, some 2,400 technical people were transferred.[11]

A year later at Grand Rapids, Michigan, UAW President R. J. Thomas estimated the engineers, designers, and draftsmen to number 4,000. The Skilled Trades Department had been charged with the responsibility of attempting to integrate and meet the special needs of this group.[12]

Most of these SDE members were incorporated with skilled-trades units in the existing industrial local unions. However, a number of miscellaneous SDE groups were also placed in the newly chartered engineering-technical Local 412 established by the UAW in June, 1943. Today this local union is one of the key units in the UAW's white-collar structure.

Integration?

That this new approach to the integration of designers—this time within production local unions—was something less than satisfactory can be inferred from the words of a subsequent publication by the Detroit Council, Society of Designing Engineers, UAW-CIO.

[10] "News Flash," Society of Designing Engineers, FAECT-CIO, July 16, 1941, p. 1, Brown Collection.

[11] UAW, *Automobile Unionism (1943). Report of President R. J. Thomas to the 8th Convention, Buffalo, N.Y.,* October 4, 1943, p. 97.

[12] UAW, *Automobile Unionism (1944). Report of President R. J. Thomas to the 9th Convention, Grand Rapids, Mich.,* September 11, 1944, p. 86.

UAW-CIO locals are vast indeed . . . cannot spend long hours working out the fine points of problems which affect only small groups . . . the six hundred engineering workers, in a local which has thirty thousand members, can hardly expect the officers to concentrate on their problems alone. . . . An engineering worker has different problems than a production worker.[13]

This need was soon recognized by President Thomas. In 1944 he announced that "engineering councils have proven a necessary adjunct in the maintenance and extension of uniform policies for our engineering members. Three councils are officially started, including Detroit, Toledo, and Flint. . . ."[14]

SDE Councils within the UAW

The coherent SDE units sought to maintain their identity and ability to deal cooperatively with the special problems of their engineering members.

According to its own publication, the Detroit Council was "primarily a clearing house for information which affects the engineering worker." It attempted to keep in touch with the Skilled Trades Division of the UAW-CIO and thus keep up with War Labor Board decisions and new legislation. It collected information on classifications, rates, apprenticeship, and upgrading. It sought more uniform standards. After collecting information, it made recommendations to the Skilled Trades Department and to the International Union. An interesting note was that "the Council acts, also, as an employment agency. . . ."[15]

Something of the distribution of SDE members in the Detroit Council can be deduced from the fact that in (approximately) 1944 the eleven Council officers included three members from Briggs Local 212, three members from Local 2, Murray Body Corporation, and two members each from Local 174 (West Side Amalgamated) and Local 190 at the Packard Motor Car Com-

---

[13] *There Was a Time* (Detroit: Detroit Council, Society of Designing Engineers, n.d.).

[14] UAW, *Automobile Unionism (1944)*, p. 86.

[15] *There Was a Time.*

pany. The sole officer from Hudson Local 154 was president.[16]

A part of Chapter 201 of the SDE had also been organized at the Detroit Controls Division of American Radiator and Standard Sanitary Corporation. This engineering and technical group was subsequently placed directly in the shop local unit which was a part of Local 174.

Interview data also indicated that a unit of the Society entered the UAW local union at Ex-Cell-O Corporation in 1945. The shop group was then a part of Local 157 and later became Local 49.[17]

Dissolution of the SDE

The newly established councils of the SDE within the UAW had a relatively short life. One early member maintained that it had become the deliberate policy of the International Union to eliminate their autonomous existence. However, another individual closely involved in SDE activity implied that membership interest simply declined and that the councils outlived their usefulness. In any event, there is no evidence of important membership protest over the abolition of the Detroit Council in 1956.[18]

Information concerning the activities of the Flint and Toledo councils is unpublished and would require field investigation to piece together the subsequent course of organization in those areas. However, it does appear that the SDE merger with the UAW industrial local unions in those locations submerged both their existence and their influence.

The Strength of an Organizing Tradition

In talking with engineering technicians in the Detroit area, I was impressed by the tenacity of an organizing tradition. Respondents made frequent references to contact with, or membership in, the old SDE. The Society appeared symbolically important

[16] *Ibid.*
[17] Interview data by author.
[18] Interview data by author.

because it represented autonomous self-organization of technical and engineering workers.

The organizing tradition represented by the Society of Designing Engineers is a definite potential asset for the UAW in organizing attempts aimed at the technical workers. Note the parallel here with the influence of the short-lived, but highly significant, employee representation plans of the National Industrial Recovery Act period.

Thus the UAW early became the beneficiary of a self-organized group of engineering technicians strategically located in the auto industry. During the later years in which this organizing among technicians was occurring, office workers in the industry began to enter the UAW—despite simultaneously existing contradictory policies which both welcomed and excluded white-collar members from full acceptance in the International Union. The conflict arising from these policies had long-lasting and, particularly at Ford, costly effects.

Quid Pro Quo

The second historical theme that can be identified in the growth of the UAW's white-collar membership was essentially negative. The International Union, with the agreement of interested local unions, was initially willing to trade the Union's white-collar organizing future for "here and now" bargaining gains for blue-collar members.

Certain deals or horse trades were negotiated with automobile management in the Union's early days. There is a general record of formal and informal exclusion of white-collar or similar groups, which at one time or another included foremen, skilled trades personnel associated with technical and engineering employees, laboratory technicians, draftsmen, and office personnel.

Two types of activities were involved: the use of explicit contract provisions to exclude white-collar workers from the Union's organizing efforts and, second, UAW repudiation of embryonic white-collar organizing interest.

Contract Clauses Excluding White-Collar Workers

The contract practice appeared quite early. Office Worker Ritter at the 1941 UAW constitutional convention commented: "We believe that if this organizing drive is accomplished there should be no further necessity of drawing up contracts with corporations which bargain the rights of the office workers away. . . ."[19]

The 1941 Ford-UAW agreement can be cited as illustrative of the practice:

> The Company recognizes the Union as the exclusive collective bargaining agency for all the employees of the Company in all of the production and assembly plants and units of the Company . . . with the exception of the following categories, which are hereby excluded:

> Superintendents . . . general foremen . . . all employees in the Sociological Department; all employees employed exclusively in the "Administration Building" (but service and maintenance employees) . . . time-study men; plant protection employees; chief engineers in power plants; designing, production, estimating and planning engineers; layout men and chemists; metallurgists; physicists; students and instructors in technical schools; artists; professional employees, their professional assistants and those training in the professions; "Dearborn" laboratory workers. . . .[20]

In 1942 the implication conveyed by the listing of excluded categories was even more explicit:

> The union agrees that it will not attempt to organize employees in the excluded categories. Employees formerly members of the Union and presently in the payroll department desiring to trans-

---

[19] UAW, *Proceedings, 1941 Convention Buffalo, N.Y.*, August 7, p. 47.

[20] *Agreement between the Ford Motor Company and the United Automobile Workers of America* (Detroit: Research Department, Ford Organizing Committee, Ford Local 600, UAW-CIO, June 20, 1941), p. 1.

fer into classifications subject to the jurisdiction of the Union will be given opportunities to make such transfers.[21]

In the 1946 agreement a listing of excluded jobs now appeared largely in Appendix B rather than in the recognition clause itself. Personnel in the administrative offices were explicitly listed, and twenty-two categories of professional employees were placed outside the Union's interest. Article I, Section 3 still specified: "The Union agrees that it will not attempt to organize employees in the excluded categories."[22]

Elimination of Contract Exclusion

Some indication of UAW restiveness with respect to this practice can be inferred from President R. J. Thomas's report to the 1946 UAW convention. He pointed out that the UAW's skilled trades department had assisted in organizing engineers where contract provisions prohibited the inclusion of such workers in existing local unions.[23]

By 1946 the exclusion issue had become important enough (perhaps because of UAW white-collar successes at Chrysler and elsewhere) for the Union to comment in a convention resolution on the organization of white-collar workers: "Be it finally resolved: That our International Executive Board stand instructed not to sign or approve any contracts which close the door on the possibility of organizing any white-collar workers."[24]

Resolutions Committee Chairman Victor Reuther attempted to clarify the resolution for the delegates: "What we are trying to prevent is the signing of contracts with clauses in them that say we will not organize workers that come within the jurisdic-

[21] *Agreement between International Union, United Automobile, Aircraft, and Agricultural Implement Workers of America (UAW-CIO) and the Ford Motor Company*, November 4, 1942, pp. 1–2.

[22] *Agreement between International Union, United Automobile, Aircraft, and Agricultural Implement Workers of America (UAW-CIO) and the Ford Motor Company*, February 26, 1946, p. 3. Also see Appendix B, pp. 72–76.

[23] UAW, *Automobile Unionism (1946). Report of President R. J. Thomas to the 10th Convention, Atlantic City, N.J.*, March 23, 1946, p. 74.

[24] UAW, *Proceedings, 10th Convention, Atlantic City, N.J.*, March 23–31, 1946, p. 39.

tion of the automobile industry. . . . We just don't think we ought to sign away the right of those white-collar workers to have a Union. In some instances, that has been done. . . ."[25]

The discussion in the *Proceedings* gave no indication of active support for the retention of such excluding clauses or of opposition to the proposal to prohibit them in future contracts. The motion to adopt the resolution was carried.

A perusal of Ford-UAW contracts subsequent to the passage of the resolution demonstrates eventual conformance with the convention's mandate.[26]

The Comparable Practice of "Stipulating Out"

Although it is not possible to cite specific instances, it seems reasonable to infer that comparable exclusions have frequently occurred at the level of individual departments and sections within other firms in the industry.

For example, within the Chrysler Corporation itself the UAW has apparently "picked and chosen" the most immediately practical dividing lines in seeking to gain NLRB election victories among white-collar workers. By a gerrymandering process doubtful groups are "stipulated out" of the particular election unit. UAW Local 889 comments:

> Historically, a white-collar unit, as certified by the National Labor Relations Board, contains a great many more exclusions from the unit than is the case in a production and maintenance unit.
>
> Management has often gone to great lengths and induced expensive hearings with innumerable delays in order to protect those jobs which they feel are "supervisory" or "confidential" in nature.
>
> In the past, in an effort to gain a consent election or an early Board decision on the appropriateness of the proposed unit, the

[25] *Ibid.*, p. 40.
[26] *Agreement between International Union, United Automobile, Aircraft, and Agricultural Implement Workers of America (UAW-CIO) and the Ford Motor Company,* August 21, 1947, p. 8.

trend has been to give up on many of those individuals to whom the management objects.[27]

Significance of Excluding Clauses

One should not exaggerate the present significance of these exclusions in UAW white-collar organizational history. However, the Union's early actions in this regard have constituted a long-term liability for the UAW in its organizing efforts in the white-collar area. This has been particularly true in Detroit (most directly at Ford), where the Union's earlier practices seem to have become a part of the membership and the public's "folklore"— often in distorted form.

This confusion appeared at a number of points in interviews when touching upon the question of future white-collar organization at Ford and General Motors. A number of respondents felt that the UAW still had some formal agreement to refrain from organizing Ford white-collar employees. Alternatively, some respondents conveyed the impression that some kind of a secret "understanding" with the company still existed. They saw this as the real reason for the white-collar "open office" conditions at Ford. Such views imply both confusion and some distrust of UAW motives. As such, they indicate the possibility that this misinformation might be exploited by either management or competing unions during organizing campaigns.

Other Types of Exclusion

A number of incidents of specific exclusions of groups actively interested in organizing can also be cited. Invariably, these seem to have left a residue of resentment in the groups affected.

For example, considerable organizing activity occurred among Ford office and technical employees both prior to and parallel with negotiation of the 1941 UAW contract. One of these incidents was later recalled at the 1946 Convention: "I recall that

[27] Wallace Webber et al., "Analysis of the White-Collar Organizational Problem: Presentation before the UAW International Executive Board (Detroit: UAW Local 889, January 20, 1960), p. 30.

in the original Ford contract the payroll department was organized and then it was cancelled out of the contract, due to some finagling . . . I recall at one time the members of the payroll department picketed the members of the International Union for being sold out."[28]

In another similar incident the CIO's Federation of Architects, Engineers, Chemists, and Technicians had conducted a successful organizing campaign among a group of Ford technical employees. In fact, the FAECT had obtained enough signed authorization cards to make possible a petition for an NLRB election. The campaign was dropped when, according to a union official personally involved, the Ford-UAW recognition agreement carried "a stipulation by Murray himself" that there was to be only one CIO international union recognized at Ford.[29]

A similar doctrine of expediency appears to have compromised the Union's relations with strategically important Ford Local 245. This local union adjoins white-collar technical and engineering groups. A union publication points out: "This defeat of the hired thugs of Harry Bennett, Henry Ford's number one hatchet man, brought about the first union shop and check-off system. Part of the price the UAW had to pay for these major concessions was the exclusion from certification of the workers in Ford Engineering, or Dearborn Laboratories as it was then known."[30] It was stated in this same source that the group had originally voted "80% for a union." The group subsequently organized under a charter granted by the Mechanics Educational Society of America (MESA). Recognition as a UAW local union was achieved in 1942.

An independent organization of metallurgists and chemists at Ford, the Fraternity of Laboratory Workers, also partly blames the UAW's rejection of their early organizing efforts for the unit's unwillingness to accept affiliation with the Autoworkers today.[31] A shift in the Fraternity's views could dramatically improve the UAW's prospects at Ford.

[28] UAW, *Proceedings, 10th Convention*, p. 41.
[29] Interview data by author.
[30] See *White-Collar Report*, no. 219, May 15, 1961, p. C-3.
[31] Interview data by author.

Success at Chrysler

4

The third historical strand to be examined and evaluated is that of office worker organizing, which centered on the Chrysler Corporation. Organizing activity here is still proceeding successfully in one unit after another.

Early Beginnings

Very early in the history of the UAW-CIO there appeared evidence of the concern, at least by a small group of members, for the potential organizing opportunity constituted by the automobile industry's white-collar employees. Among the issues submitted by various local unions for the consideration of the delegates to the UAW's second convention at Milwaukee in 1937 was Resolution Number 146. It was entitled "Resolution on the Organization of Office Workers in the Auto Industry." The sponsor was A. Richards of Local Union Number 262, a Detroit local with 2,200 members.[1]

It is interesting to note the context of this resolution. The International Union had been growing dramatically. President Homer Martin reported that the 30,000 members of a year earlier had now become 300,000.[2] Thus it is somewhat surpris-

---

[1] See "Resolutions Submitted by Various Local Unions," Appendix III, UAW, *Second Annual Convention, Milwaukee, Wis.,* August 23–28, 1937, p. 70.

[2] A more conservative estimate shows a membership of 27,058 in 1936 and one of 231,894 in 1937—however, this is "average dues-paying member-

ing that even passing attention would be devoted to the white-collar issue. The problems of assimilation and administration connected with such an expansion must have been tremendous.

White-Collar Workers Begin to Speak

White-collar members acquired their own voice in 1941. In that year newly chartered Industrial Office Workers' Amalgamated Local 889 first sent two representatives, Truzel and Ritter, to the International UAW-CIO Convention in Buffalo.

> This, I believe, is the first time in the history of the U.A.W. (C.I.O.) that an office worker in the automobile field was given a voice at an International Convention. . . . On the very eve of this great convention we were granted a charter . . . and we are now known as Office Workers' Local No. 889, U.A.W. (C.I.O.) Today we are one week old. This is the beginning of a tremendous job. . . .[3]

Optimism was the keynote. Ritter felt that "an organizational drive would give the necessary impetus to the upwards of 70,000 unorganized workers who are crying for organization." Given some good organizers, "We can and we will complete the job within the next six months." In fact, the white-collar workers were "now on the fence and all they need is one little shove to put them on our side." The resolution in question was then unanimously passed.

A favorable organizing trend at the time can also be inferred from the fact that the Union's primary publication, *The United Automobile Worker,* published a one-issue "white-collar edition" on April 15, 1941. The front page carried an application for membership. Other UAW members were assured that "Office Workers throughout the nation are watching the rapid development of the Association of Office Workers."[4]

---

ship." Even by this measure the Union gained over 200,000 members in that period. See UAW, *Report of Emil Mazey, International Secretary-Treasurer, 18th Constitutional Convention, Atlantic City, N.J.,* May 4–10, 1962, p. 5.

[3] UAW, *Proceedings, 1941 Convention, Buffalo, N.Y.,* August 7, pp. 45–46.

[4] "White-Collar Edition," *United Automobile Worker,* Detroit, April 15, 1941, p. 1.

GOSHEN COLLEGE LIBRARY
GOSHEN, INDIANA 46526

The First Victory at Chrysler

According to company records the first organized office in the Chrysler Corporation was established just outside the Detroit area. The Marysville (Michigan) Parts Depot office was organized by the UAW in December, 1941, and became Local 954. The local union had a membership of between one and two hundred. President Thomas reported to the seventh UAW convention that "the office workers of the Marysville, Michigan, plant voted 95% CIO in the first election of this sort in the automobile industry."[5]

The convention subsequently passed Resolution Number 31, "On Organizational Activities":

> Whereas: The International Constitution of the UAW-CIO under Article 5, relative to "Jurisdiction" includes among those eligible for membership "employees engaged in office work, sales, distribution and maintenance thereof" as pertaining to farm, automobile, aircraft, agricultural implements; and

> Whereas: There are upwards of a million persons employed in the automotive service industry in these classifications with less than ten thousand of these persons organized in the UAW-CIO. . . .

> Therefore be it resolved: That the delegates . . . go on record as instructing the incoming International Executive Board to take all the necessary steps possible to organize all these various industries and all other unorganized plants.[6]

From the Marysville Parts Depot "beachhead" the UAW organizing activity spread widely through the corporation. Including technical units in numbers roughly equal to office-clerical members, the Union eventually represented a total of 8,500 Chrysler white-collar workers by 1958.[7] Ten years later, with

[5] UAW, *Automobile Unionism* (*1943*). *Report of President R. J. Thomas to the 7th Convention, Chicago, Ill.*, August 3, 1942, p. 27.
[6] UAW, *Proceedings, 7th Convention, Chicago, Ill.*, August 3–9, 1942, pp. 364–365.
[7] See *White-Collar Report*, no. 104, March 2, 1959, pp. A-7 to A-8.

counterbalancing trends of unit erosion and new organizing largely offsetting each other, the Union continued to represent some 8,000 Chrysler white-collar employees.

The Chrysler breakthrough has probably been the single most important asset of the UAW in the white-collar field. It resulted in an indispensable concentration of white-collar workers that became the base for all later white-collar efforts of the Union. And it provided the Union with the very useful concept of organizing "along the corporate chain," which seems to constitute one of the most productive white-collar approaches.

However, the Union was still acting primarily as a passive receiver, as it had with the SDE units. Early organization at Chrysler was much more a result of management ineptness than of UAW facility in organizing.

Although the Union should be credited with sufficient astuteness to accept the opportunity offered, the primary enabling element was the Chrysler management's neglect and mishandling of white-collar employees. Briefly stated, the company's mistakes in this regard included a chaotic white-collar rate structure and job classification system. Merit increases were widely misused by supervisors. Favoritism, arbitrary promotions, demotions, and discharges and salary "secrecy" were prominent features of the white-collar worker's life at Chrysler.[8]

White-Collar vs. Blue-Collar

From 1941 to 1957 sporadic interest in organizing the white-collar group was expressed by UAW convention resolutions. However, there was little indication of important rank-and-file blue-collar worker concern for expanding white-collar membership. In fact, there was some suggestion that, where the blue-collar silence did not signify apathy, it contained a component of distrust and dislike. This arose from the clerical and technical workers' occasional snobbishness and their willingness to cross picket lines during blue-collar strikes.

[8] In interviews both management and union representatives volunteered, "The company was the union's best organizer."

For example, Delegate England at the 1947 convention of the Union stated: "We also feel that the Local Unions have a very definite stake; that it is demoralizing when a strike takes place and office workers try to cross the picket lines."[9]

Another explicit statement of this problem is also found in Resolution Number 5, "Organization of White-Collar Workers," submitted to the tenth Convention of the UAW at Atlantic City in 1946. "In recent strikes efforts have been made to pit the unorganized white-collar workers against the organized workers. . . ."[10]

Such incidents must have been accompanied by an increasing blue-collar recognition of the white-collar organizing potential. At the same time, though, the UAW's slowly growing white-collar membership was probably regarded with mixed emotions by both rank-and-file blue-collar members and the leadership of the International Union.

Ford's "Open Office"

Once the Union had achieved an increasingly secure white-collar base at a major auto company such as Chrysler, Ford and General Motors became the logical targets for UAW organizing efforts. Yet by 1972 the Union had still been markedly unsuccessful in following up its gains at Chrysler with entry into the balance of the auto industry.

White-collar organization at the Ford Motor Company has been plagued by a series of incidents which have generally favored the company's "open office" policy. These have tended to discourage the unionization of significant numbers of either office or technical workers by any major "outside" union.

The most limiting influence at Ford has been that stemming from the UAW's unfortunate agreement initially to exclude engineering and technical, as well as office-clerical, personnel from organizational attempts through its early contracts and informal

[9] UAW, *Proceedings, 11th Convention, Atlantic City, N.J.,* November 9–14, 1947, p. 74.
[10] UAW, *Proceedings, 10th Convention, Atlantic City N.J.,* March 23–31, 1946, p. 41.

agreements with the company in the 1940's. Although the formal damage has since been repaired by removing the excluding clause from the labor agreement, the effects of this concession by the UAW are still discernible.

Skilled-trades Local 245, the natural base for an extension of unionization among technical and engineering personnel at Ford, was by its own admission unable to do more than defend its existing position in 1961. This incapacity can be charged directly to the confusion and resentment created by its original exclusion from the UAW and from Local 600.

The independent Fraternity of Laboratory Workers, which was discussed above in connection with the organization of technicians, represented another potential foothold for the Union. However, it, too, originated as a group of technicians who were similarly excluded from the UAW. The Fraternity has, therefore, been generally unwilling to affiliate with the International Union.

Union Unreadiness

After contract exclusion was repaired, the UAW was still unready to move effectively against Ford. Thus in the 1940's the Union missed its prime opportunity to represent white-collar workers at two of the three major auto producers. Two such organizing opportunities can be identified. In the period of company degeneration (before Vice-President Ernest Breech introduced his series of famous, thoroughgoing renovations beginning in 1945), as well as during the unsettling period of basic reorganization that followed Breech's appointment, the UAW was completely unprepared to mount a major organizing drive. During a recentralization phase in 1958 considerable white-collar unrest again developed. The Union was no more foresighted than before.[11]

A number of organizing attempts have been made by the

---

[11] This point was emphasized by an employer representative (non-Ford) in an interview with me. For an account of the intensive reorganization of the company, see "The Rebirth of Ford," *Fortune,* May, 1947, pp. 82–89, 204–211.

UAW at Ford. As early as 1947 a campaign at the Lincoln-Mercury plant in Dearborn resulted in a 254 to 62 vote against the Union. In 1957 a UAW drive at Ford's Canton, Ohio, plant failed even to reach the election stage.[12]

Continued probing in the Union's post-1965 campaign at several Ford locations yielded only one near victory. At the corporation's Cleveland stamping plant, the unit voted 74 to 62 against representation. The vote at a technicians' unit at the Dearborn Engineering facility in May, 1968, was less encouraging to the Union. The UAW received 323 votes, compared to a total of 722 votes for no union.[13]

Then, in a rather surprising turn of events, an in-plant independent union, the Society of Engineering Office Workers, won representation rights for 1,010 design and office employees at Ford's Dearborn engineering center in February, 1970. The vote was 511 to 498, in contrast to the group's 1968 rejection of the UAW by 722 to 323. The SEOW demonstrated increasing support by winning a decertification election vote, 532 to 426.[14]

Fortress GM

A major segment of unorganized white-collar autoworkers exists at the General Motors Corporation. Yet, despite having obtained several small organizing footholds over the years, the UAW's efforts here have been remarkably well contained by the company.

The primary penetration by the Society of Designing Engineers in the 1930's in General Motors in Flint and Detroit was followed by gains in formal National Labor Relations Board elections at least as late as 1941.[15] However, the original SDE organization failed to expand in Detroit-area General Motors

---

[12] Interview data by author.

[13] See *White-Collar Report,* no. 477, April 28, 1966, p. A-8, and no. 586, May 30, 1968, pp. A-7 to A-8.

[14] *White-Collar Report,* no. 691, June 5, 1970, p. A-10; no. 693, June 19, 1970, pp. A-7 to A-8; no. 737, April 23, 1971, pp. A-3 to A-4.

[15] "News Flash," Society of Designing Engineers, FAECT-CIO, July 2, 1941, p. 1, Brown Collection.

plants. At Flint at least one group of draftsmen eventually voted for decertification, and one other unsuccessful attempt at decertification was made among former SDE units.

After leaving the Federation of Architects, Engineers, Chemists, and Technicians as a part of the SDE merger with the UAW-CIO, the Fisher Body Die Design unit entered Local 412. In 1957 they voted to move to Local 160, partly because they felt they were "outnumbered by Chrysler people."[16]

Since then Local 160, together with the International Union, has intermittently attempted to organize salaried groups at the huge GM Technical Center. A union drive among styling personnel was unsuccessful in October, 1958. A similar attempt aimed at photographic workers also failed in 1959. However, the UAW did meet with success a year later among plastics workers holding salaried status. The Union claimed at the time that "these UAW members are the only ones in the auto industry who have the Stock Thrift Plan."[17]

Union Membership and Salaried Status at General Motors

The Union maintains that one of the reasons for the lack of white-collar organization here has been the company's ability to divide salaried and hourly workers against each other. "General Motors . . . has developed to a fine art the employment of many salaried enticements to undermine UAW organizing drives."[18]

In earlier years at the corporation unionization was the signal for immediate removal from salaried status—a fairly important value in the mind of the white-collar employee. In exchange for a company bargaining concession, the Fisher Die Design unit voluntarily chose to accept hourly status. After an adverse National Labor Relations Board ruling, the company later was no longer able to unilaterally change units to hourly status. Nevertheless, the precedent of the former practice seems to have left

[16] Interview data by author.
[17] See "Local 160—General Motors Technical Center," *White-Collar Report*, no. 219, May 15, 1961, pp. C-2 to C-3.
[18] *Ibid.*

General Motors employees with a strong belief that the loss of salaried standing is a nearly inevitable consequence of joining the Union. The issue still remains in controversy.[19]

In June, 1970, continued strong opposition by the General Motors management was credited with the defeat of an organizing attempt by 1,164 production engineering employees of the company's Central Engineering Plant of the Fisher Body Division in Warren, Michigan. Significantly, self-organization emerged from an in-plant independent union. The vote was 596 to 317 against unionization.[20] In January, 1972, the UAW lost another attempt among a group of payroll auditors at a Cleveland GM installation by a vote of 28 to 18.[21]

White-Collar Members in Supplier Firms

Although important organizing potential exists in the numerous supplier firms in the auto industry, the diversity and geographical spread of these companies makes generalization difficult. However, the earliest instance of office worker organization in the entire automobile industry probably occurred at a supplier firm, the Kelsey-Hayes Company, in 1937–38.

Perhaps because of the economic pressure for cost reduction applied by the Big Three customers, the supplier firms have tended to offer organizing opportunities more readily than have Ford and General Motors. However, it is also true that these firms, by virtue of their smaller size, generally have less systematic programs of personnel administration to counter unionizing efforts.

The supplier firms do confirm the general workability of the "corporate chain" approach to organizing which we have identified at Chrysler. Multi-location firms, such as the Dana Cor-

[19] See "In re General Motors Corporation (Linden, N.J.) and Federation of Architects, Engineers, Chemists, and Technicians, Chapter 31 (CIO)," Case no. 2–6–5385, December 19, 1944, 59 *NLRB* 1143. In 1970 the UAW was still demanding that the Fisher design unit be returned to salaried status. See *White-Collar Report,* no. 698, July 24, 1970, pp. A-3 to A-4.

[20] *White-Collar Report,* no. 693, June 19, 1970, pp. A-7 to A-8.

[21] *White-Collar Report,* no. 774, January 14, 1972, p. A-3.

poration and Budd Company, are cases in point. Each has numerous white-collar UAW units.

Finally, remember that white-collar technicians in supplier firms were often active in the Society of Designing Engineers. With the Society's transfer to the UAW these technicians became functioning members of the Union. Usually the SDE chapters became somewhat autonomous units within the production locals or were attached to amalgamated local unions of production workers.

Aerospace and Agriculture

Sizable blocks of white-collar UAW members exist in the aerospace and agricultural implement portions of the Union's jurisdiction, as noted earlier. Only a very limited mention of these groups can be made at this point, because comparable interview materials were not accessible, nor could published materials be found which were useful in this connection.

Many of the UAW membership gains in the aircraft industry have been made integrally with the organization of production workers. This seems to result from the close association of engineering and technical workers with the high proportion of skilled labor required by the industry. There is a much hazier line of demarcation between white- and blue-collar members here than in the other two UAW industries. However, an important exception exists in the Curtiss-Wright local union, which is clearly identifiable as white-collar. This local has served as an active center for the Union's white-collar activities in its eastern region.

A similar center has developed at International Harvester, where most of the UAW's agricultural implement white-collar office and technical people are located.[22]

There is very little published information about white-collar organization in the implement industry. The beginning of the concentration of UAW white-collar membership at Harvester derived from earlier organization of office workers by the United Office and Public Workers. Subsequent defection of these local

[22] *UAW TOP Reporter,* July–August, 1967, p. 3.

unions to the UAW followed the controversy over Communist domination. Thus Delegate Noel from Harvester Local 305 stated from the floor at the thirteenth convention in 1951: "We, at Harvester, belonged to the UOPWA for a period of approximately five years. We got sick of the policies . . . connected with every Communist Party organization in the United States. . . ."[23]

White-Collar Coalescence

In terms of an analogy, the white-collar group in the UAW had acquired sufficient size by the late 1950's to constitute a critical mass for internal political purposes.

The event which seems to have crystallized the white-collar bloc into a working political coalition was their successful execution of a national strike effort against the Chrysler Corporation in 1958. It consisted of a six-day stoppage by office and technical workers.

The strike came as the culmination of persisting disagreements during an extended period of contract negotiations. Some 8,000 employees were involved, mainly in the Detroit area. About 20 percent of the strikers were women, according to an estimate by *Detroit News* reporter Asher Lauren.[24] Although production workers honored the picket lines, the withdrawal of the office function alone was adequate to force production to cease.[25] All available evidence indicates that the strike was well organized, that membership support and participation were everything that the Union might have desired, and that the UAW's tactic exerted effective pressure upon the company.

The strike clearly verified that white-collar economic action

[23] UAW, *Proceedings, 13th Constitutional Convention, Cleveland, Ohio,* April 1–6, 1951, p. 302.
[24] Asher Lauren, "Eight Chrysler Plants Shut by White-Collar Strike," *Detroit News,* November 11, 1958, pp. 1, 12.
[25] For example, a company spokesman was cited as saying, "The plants would be forced to shut down by this afternoon if the salaried workers went on strike because operations would become too confused without them." See "Pickets at Chrysler Plant," *Port Huron Times Herald,* November 11, 1958, p. 1.

was entirely practical, using a weapon familiar—if not sacred —to blue-collar members and leaders.

The Meaning of the Strike

Interview materials indicated that the impact of the strike upon white-collar opinion in the Detroit area was limited. Nevertheless, it constituted a historic transition in UAW internal white-collar affairs.

The strike paid important dividends in improved morale and self-regard among the white-collar local union leaders involved. More generally, it laid at rest an old doubt (and blue-collar skepticism) as to whether office and technical people in the auto industry would actually strike and picket like production workers. Both white-collar local union and blue-collar International Union leaders were not at all certain that this would prove true. It also appears that the UAW's president, Walter Reuther, was personally impressed by the white-collar group's bargaining during the negotiations in which he directly participated. Thus the strike signaled a coming of age for UAW white-collar leaders and members.

Why Chrysler?

In conclusion, a specific consideration of the differences in the UAW's white-collar performance at the three major auto companies is essential.

It is likely that white-collar workers in the automobile industry could have been successfully organized on a mass basis in the 1930's. However, the union was preoccupied with consolidating its position with the production and maintenance workers of the industry in those years.

Because of widespread discontent with the Chrysler Corporation's administration of white-collar employees, the UAW rather inadvertently—and without significant company opposition— established a significant bloc of office and technical members in that company by the early 1940's. This example served as a sharp warning to both Ford and General Motors. From that point onward both companies have made systematic efforts to minimize sources of white-collar dissatisfaction among their office and technical employees. Rationalized personnel policies were comprehensively applied. The seniority criterion was voluntarily followed in most instances. There has been a careful "passing along" of the monetary and benefit packages negotiated by the UAW for its blue-collar members to office and technical workers. And both Ford and General Motors have met all of the UAW's specific organizing thrusts with determined opposition, using every means at their disposal to prevent a significant union breakthrough.

The UAW's White-Collar Program: Trials and Errors, 1941–61

5

The UAW has been outstanding among American unions in its ability to project an image of creative innovation and progressiveness. Yet until 1961 the UAW's activities in the white-collar field were markedly pedestrian. The record shows a very human series of trial-and-error attempts to deal with an unfamiliar area. The Union initially made a rather reluctant adjustment to the presence and needs of a new type of member, and to the associated organizing possibilities.

Little and Late: The International Union and the White-Collar Trend

A useful approach in evaluating the response of the UAW to the problem posed by the white-collar drift is to examine the historical acts of "International"—that is, the leadership and staff above the local union level. Here authority and responsibility reside in full-time employees of the International Union. Here basic decisions concerning the allocation of funds and personnel are primarily made. Recommendations for consideration by the Union's conventions and an important influencing of convention actions both originate with this group.

An examination of the leadership role played by the International Union's elected officers and associated staff members leads to the conclusion that a largely passive pattern was followed in the white-collar area until 1961. Throughout the twenty years of significant UAW membership gains among white-collar workers, the developing white-collar bloc intermittently pressed for more decisive action. The International responded by temporizing delays and minor concessions. There was no evidence of aggressive, top-level leadership toward a broad-scale white-collar organizing effort.

As early as 1937, at the UAW's second convention, a delegate introduced a "Resolution on the Organization of Office Workers in the Auto Industry."[1] After the passage of a similar resolution at the 1941 convention a revealing exchange took place between Delegate Novak of Local 7 and President R. J. Thomas. The delegate sought additional reassurance that what had been resolved would, in fact, be carried out. The developing pattern of the white-collar group's push for action and the International Union's considerably more restrained enthusiasm can be discerned in President Thomas's reply: "I considered that by the unanimous support of this convention the thing you have requested has been done . . . I don't know what else to do. The whole convention stood up. I can't pull up the floor, too."[2]

When?

At Atlantic City in 1947 in the eleventh convention white-collar delegates gave clear expression of impatience with the Union's progress in organizing. It appears from the *Proceedings* that white-collar locals had submitted a resolution that was subsequently "restated" by the Resolutions Committee. Delegate Skinner expressed appreciation for the effort of the Resolutions Committee "in submitting something in our behalf." But delegate Erickson of Local 889 was more blunt. "I don't think the resolution of the Resolutions Committee is going to do us much good. . . . There has been no organizational drive whatever for this union. . . ." He much preferred the original resolution.

[1] See "Resolutions Submitted by Various Local Unions," Appendix III, UAW, *Second Annual Convention, Milwaukee, Wis.,* August 23–28, 1937, p. 70.

[2] UAW, *Proceedings, 1941 Convention, Buffalo, N.Y.,* August 7, p. 55.

"I believe if our resolution . . . was passed in its entirety . . . we would get somewhere."[3]

The 1949 Milwaukee convention saw the proposing of Resolution Number 21, "Organization of Office Workers." The resolution claimed that "some progress" had been made since the previous convention. However, Local 889 Delegate Johnston observed: "Year after year, since 1942, we have come to conventions and presented resolutions for your consideration. We believe that over a period of time these conventions are beginning to accept the fact that they must organize office workers."[4]

The failure of white-collar members to secure action on their recommendations can be traced partly to their inconsequential voting power and minority position among the mass of blue-collar members. For example, Jack Stieber found that office and technical workers constituted only 2 percent of the delegates to the 1959 UAW Convention.[5] Thus this group was decidedly underrepresented in relation to its share in the total UAW membership, as approximately 5 percent of the Union was white collar.

But for many of the early years these failures probably also derived from a lack of leadership and know-how adequate for the highly political environment in which they found themselves. Except for attempts such as those just described, white-collar members took only a very limited role in general convention activities. At the Cleveland convention in 1951 there were no separate resolutions on the white-collar problem. The extent of white-collar participation in the affairs of the convention can be inferred from the remarks of Delegate Noel: "During the whole Convention proceedings I have not heard a delegate in support of the office workers or speak for the office workers. I feel that something should be said in support of the office workers."[6]

[3] UAW, *Proceedings, 11th Convention, Atlantic City, N.J.,* November 9–14, 1947, pp. 70–71.
[4] UAW, *Proceedings, 12th Convention, Milwaukee, Wis.,* July 10–15, 1949, p. 31.
[5] Jack Stieber, *Governing the UAW* (New York: John Wiley and Sons, 1962), p. 18.
[6] UAW, *Proceedings, 13th Constitutional Convention, Cleveland, Ohio,* April 1–6, 1951, p. 302.

Formation of White-Collar Department

In President Walter Reuther's report to the fourteenth convention in 1953 one of the few positive acts of the top leadership in the white-collar area was announced. The International Union had established an Office Workers Department within the UAW's administrative structure.[7]

However, four year later President Reuther's 1957 report demonstrated the International Union's increasingly serious interest in white-collar organizing. Beyond the usual report of the (by then) Office and Technical Workers Department, a separate three-page section discussed "Organization and Membership Growth" as connected with the issues in "White-Collar, Technical, Engineer Organizing."[8]

The Significance of Honeywell

In the record of the 1957 convention two important historical events related to the white-collar theme. The first of these was the attempt to enhance the UAW's position in its struggle to retain the support of the independently organized Federation of Honeywell Engineers. The Federation had only recently affiliated with the UAW and was wavering dangerously toward decertification. The second occurrence was a fundamental modification in the constitutional structure of the Union.

The convention was chosen as the place for a public charter presentation ceremony—an extraordinary use of convention time. This was to highlight the significance of the Honeywell organization to the UAW's future in organizing engineers and technicians—and, it appears, to help swing votes among the undecided group at Honeywell at the same time![9]

The decertification which ultimately took place proved a sharp,

[7] UAW, *Report of President Walter P. Reuther to the 14th Convention, Atlantic City, N.J.*, March 22, 1953, pp. 171–172.

[8] UAW, *Report of President Walter P. Reuther to the 16th Constitutional Convention, Atlantic City, N.J.*, April 7–12, 1957, pp. 217–219.

[9] UAW, *Proceedings, 16th Constitutional Convention, Atlantic City, N.J.*, April 7–12, 1957, p. 365.

if not disastrous, setback to UAW aspirations in the professional engineering field. On the basis of interview studies both before and after the decertification election it is probable that nothing the UAW could have done in the inadequate time available could have salvaged the group. The situation was a near classic case of historically generated internal conflicts, confused membership attitudes, and effective company exploitation of these elements.[10]

In retrospect, it seems that UAW success at Minneapolis-Honeywell could have "started the ball rolling" among engineers on a national scale. It can also be reasonably speculated that such a victory would have encouraged the doubters among the UAW's own leaders, and it would have given strong support to the group within the UAW that has called for more vigorous action and a substantial expenditure of funds for white-collar organization. Thus the Honeywell defeat may well have caused the postponement of major UAW effort in the white-collar field for a considerable number of years.

Structural Change in the UAW

The second event at the 1957 convention related to the Union's increasing concern for white-collar organization was a fundamental modification of its constitution. The change allowed certain groups of workers to have increased autonomy and separate representation in dealing with their unique problems.

The amendment with respect to the ratification of labor agreements read:

> Upon application to and approval of the International Executive Board, a ratification procedure may be adopted wherein apprenticeable skilled trades and related workers, production workers, office workers, engineers, and technicians would vote

[10] See University of Minnesota Industrial Relations Center, *Report of Findings on Attitudes, Communications, and Participation of Honeywell Engineers* (Minneapolis: University of Minnesota Industrial Relations Center, 1957) and Everett Taft and Gregory P. Stone, "An Unpublished Study of the Voting Record and Attitudes of the Minneapolis Federation of Engineers Who Were Surveyed by Mail during the Month Following the National Labor Relations Board Decertification Election, May 8, 1957."

on contractual matters which related exclusively to each group. All members of the Local Union would continue to vote as one unit on matters that are common to all members of the Local Union.[11]

The representation change was stated thus:

> Upon application to and approval of the International Executive Board, stewards and/or committeemen may be elected exclusively by and from appropriate groups . . . in keeping with the policy resolution adopted by the Sixteenth Constitutional Convention.[12]

Such provisions as these are of key importance to white-collar members in an industrial union to guarantee special attention to their problems and a voice in determining their own destiny. Yet this proposal provoked hardly any debate directed specifically at the white-collar issue. The faction opposed to the proposed change believed that the Union might be weakened by the inherent modification of the industrial union principle. It also resented what it charged was primarily an appeasement of the dissident skilled tradesmen. Thus debate followed those lines.

Quieting the Doubts

Vice-President Leonard Woodcock was assigned the task of carrying the day for the administration's viewpoint. He attempted to place the constitutional change in a framework broader than simply that of the skilled-trades dispute:

> This is being talked about as the Skilled Trades Program. It deals obviously with the skilled trades problem, but it is infinitely more than that, and it is our very fervent opinion that the future of this Union as an effective instrument is on trial in these minutes through which this Convention is now passing.

---

[11] UAW, *Proceedings, 16th Convention*, p. 275. Also see *Constitution of the International Union, United Automobile, Aerospace, and Agricultural Implement Workers of America, UAW*, adopted at Atlantic City, N.J., March, 1964, p. 39.

[12] UAW, *Proceedings, 16th Convention*, p. 275.

We are also concerned with two other vital groups in our in-dustries, the engineers and technicians and the office workers.[13]

The final three-fourths of his presentation (approximately three printed pages) was devoted to the highly controversial skilled-trades dilemma of the UAW and to refuting the "craft unionism" charge. His concluding remarks indicated the ad-ministration's evaluation of the gravity of the situation.

> If you grant us this leverage we can capture and we can keep the initiative in 1958 and the years after. If you do not, we believe that our Union can well be on the way to a second-class status. The leadership team has given this long, sober and careful consideration. We are absolutely convinced that these changes are most necessary. We urge—I use again the words "we beg"—your approval to keep UAW as an effective fighting force to make UAW more effective to meet the great chal-lenges which lie ahead.[14]

Significantly for our concern here, the sharp and protracted debate which followed (taking up some eighteen pages of printed comment in the *Proceedings*) was concerned solely with the skilled-trades issue. None was directed at, or critical of, the white-collar implications discussed by Vice-President Wood-cock.[15]

When debate closed, the administration-backed change was approved by at least 95 percent of the delegates. Either for reasons of strategy or because of apathy the debate showed no evidence of any inclination by white-collar delegates to enter the discussion.

At the 1966 Long Beach convention the UAW continued to move toward a greater degree of structural differentiation by providing that the groups dealt with above "would vote sepa-rately on contractual matters common to all and, in the same vote, on those matters which related exclusively to their group."[16]

[13] *Ibid.*, p. 280.
[14] *Ibid.*, p. 284.
[15] *Ibid.*, pp. 284–304.
[16] UAW, *Proceedings, 20th Constitutional Convention, Long Beach, Calif.*, May 16–21, 1966, p. 405.

Executive Board Inaction

Despite the newly devised structural potential the UAW's Executive Board took little action on the white-collar problem from 1957 to 1959. "Resolution No. 23, Organizing the Engineers, Technicians and Office and Clerical Workers" was referred to the Board by the 1959 convention. Newspapers subsequently reported the restructuring of the Union's organizational activities under a single director. An Associated Press news item indicated that the UAW was seeking "a million new members."[17]

However, these efforts in attracting white-collar members seemed increasingly unsuccessful. A summary contained in *White-Collar Report* showed the UAW winning four white-collar elections (involving 45 employees) and losing ten elections (involving 1,900 white collar employees) during 1960. In 1961 the UAW won two National Labor Relations Board white-collar contests to gain bargaining rights for 20 new employees. It lost eleven such elections involving 650 potential members in the same year.[18]

Having traced through union documents the general outlines of the UAW's official response to the white-collar problem until 1961, let us now look at evidence of the results of these policies and actions as they appeared in interviews just prior to that date.

Union Accomplishments

After twenty years of exposure to white-collar characteristics and needs, certain significant internal changes and assets of the UAW developed. It is my thesis that in 1961 these strengths were still more than overshadowed by weaknesses, and that this inadequacy resulted in a white-collar rank-and-file movement which subsequently achieved a fundamental renovation and redirection of the Union's white-collar affairs. However, these

[17] See, for example, "UAW Seeks Million New Members," *Ann Arbor News,* January 23, 1960, p. 2.
[18] See *White-Collar Report,* no. 205, February 6, 1961, pp. B-1 to B-2, and no. 259, February 22, 1962, pp. B-1 to B-3.

crucial gains could not have been made unless certain foundations had been laid earlier.

By 1961 the UAW had secured several important assets for future white-collar organizing. By historical good fortune it had acquired a sizable number of white-collar members in each of the Union's three industries and with wide geographic distribution. In the process the Union had developed a basic minimum of know-how in organizing and servicing these members.

White- and Blue-Collar Relations

A remarkable UAW accomplishment has been its leaders' ability to moderate earlier blue-collar resentment of the white-collar workers and to maintain an essential unity. It would have been easy for the administration to have mishandled the group relations involved. An open split and highly antagonistic attitudes on the part of both groups could have occurred. Here, the industrial union philosophy, in its emphasis upon the need for solidarity, constituted a most constructive influence.

Interviews with active white-collar union leaders and members in 1960–61 showed a surprisingly high quality of relations between white- and blue-collar workers within the Union. In view of white-collar agitation for important changes in the organization's approach to white-collar affairs, it might at first be assumed that this discontent originated in irritation at the treatment received from blue-collar-dominated locals and the International Union. On the contrary, 69 percent of active white-collar unionists interviewed described blue-collar/white-collar relations as very good or showing a high degree of cooperation on common problems. Fourteen percent thought these relations were fair. The remainder were split between "no occasion for contact" and "sometimes good, sometimes poor."

That this experience has been generally satisfactory is likewise confirmed by interview materials from inactive white-collar union members. These members indicated a decidedly lessened preference for a solely white-collar union than did unorganized white-collar workers.

Despite white-collar local union leaders' impatience with the International Union's very limited allocation of effort and resources to white-collar affairs, the leadership of the UAW had been able to establish and retain an effective relationship with the white-collar membership.

Interviews also showed high esteem among both organized and unorganized white-collar workers for the most prominent personal symbol of the UAW, President Walter Reuther. A confirmation of interview findings appeared in this comment by a white-collar local union newswriter:

> There is no doubt that the UAW enjoys certain advantages [in appealing to white-collar workers], the Reuther image among white-collars opposed to organization is a good image— he is honest, diligent and doing a good job for those he represents—these are the grudging admissions of unorganized white-collars. When you sound them out on "UAW" they usually will admit that it is a clean and democratic organization. When you try just "union," then you will likely get reactions of "strike happy" racketeers or other McClellan images.[19]

The external political action program of the Union, while less acceptable to the typical white-collar member than to the blue-collar membership, had been sufficiently explained and translated so that it was not an exploitable issue or source of schism between blue- and white-collar members.

A Workable Structure

Although deficient in ways which will be catalogued below, the Office and Technical Department (established in 1953) was at least a minimum structural facility. It offered the white-collar membership a reference point, some visibility within the Union, a partially specialized competence in white-collar organizing and servicing, and an explicit budget. The Department represented a beginning from which an improved white-collar effort might be mounted.

The constitutional change in contract ratification and repre-

[19] See *UAW Local 412 Engineering Leader,* April 26, 1962, p. 10.

sentation in 1957 offered an opening for the white-collar group to achieve autonomy and greater visibility within the International Union.

Autonomy or Integration?

A basic philosophical dilemma faces the industrial union interested in extending its white-collar membership. It must decide between the two alternatives: preservation of white-collar "difference" through autonomy, or an opposite attempt to minimize (and perhaps eventually eliminate) such distinctions through integration with blue-collar groups.

Examples of both philosophies can be found in the UAW's approach to white-collar workers. Locals 412 and 889 were chartered to include technical and office employees, respectively. In 1954 former Briggs Corporation office workers organized. They later voted, in a specially conducted election, to affiliate with the production and maintenance group, Local 212, rather than with the amalgamated office workers' Local 889. This is one of the few instances where white-collar members have expressed a specific preference for inclusion in a blue-collar unit, despite the availability of an alternative white-collar affiliation. However, the Briggs unit seems very satisfied with its initial choice. Although considerable white-collar autonomy is exercised within the local union, the overall emphasis is much more strongly upon integral solidarity with blue-collar members than in the typical UAW situation.

It appears that local structuring of white-collar units during the first twenty years of UAW white-collar experience was largely haphazard. There was no consistent attempt to provide white-collar autonomy. Yet, in balance, the Union slowly moved toward a more frequent designation of consciously white-collar units.

The 1958 White-Collar Strike

The 1958 white-collar strike at the Chrysler Corporation became an important milestone in the maturation of the white-collar group as trade unionists, as mentioned above. In interviews, the successful execution of this traditional trade union "baptism of fire" rite was interpreted by active white-collar union members in primarily noneconomic terms.

Thus 42 percent of the interviewees stated that the strike was "useful in building the morale of white-collar units and members." That the strike "demonstrated white-collar organizational effectiveness to the company" was the opinion of 29 percent of those interviewed. And 17 percent felt that the strike "created considerably greater respect by management for white-collar units." Other comments indicated that the strike "improved white-collar standing in the eyes of blue-collar locals" or that it "demonstrated white-collar spirit and unity to the International Union." Only 12 percent indicated that the strike made important economic gains or prevented important economic losses.

Unfinished Business

The Union's assets by 1961 have been summarized. Now for a look at its liabilities.

The stalemate in white-collar organizing reflected by the previously cited 1960 and 1961 election results can be traced to a number of weaknesses in the UAW's approach to the white-collar problem. These deficiencies have since been successfully attacked and remedied, at least in part, by significant changes in the Union's methods, as channeled through the Technical-Office-Professional Department (formed in 1962). But where this is not true, these points offer the possibility of additional improvement in the future. In both cases many of these errors or weaknesses are inherently typical of industrial union approaches in the white-collar field. Thus it becomes highly relevant to consider these deficiencies in order to evaluate the possibility of industrial union white-collar expansion in the future.

Limited Allocation of Union Resources

The agency within the UAW that was primarily responsible for white-collar affairs, the Office and Technical Department, was allocated very limited funds, staff, and talent. A rough measure of the Union's commitment to white-collar expansion was its spending for this department, as summarized in Table 5–1.

Although the actual dollars spent have some usefulness in indicating the absolute size of the UAW's efforts in the white-collar

TABLE 5–1. SELECTED UAW EXPENDITURES, 1946–61

Period Covered	Office & Technical	% of All Department Expenditures
Nov. 30, 1946—May 31, 1947	4,610.50	0.3
June 1, 1948—May 31, 1949	24,367.64	0.7
June 1, 1949—May 31, 1950	24,858.89	0.6
June 1, 1950—May 31, 1951	17,660.33	0.4
*June 1, 1951—May 31, 1952	64,826.03	0.9
*June 1, 1952—Nov. 30, 1952	35,350.78	1.0
*Jan. 1, 1953—June 30, 1953	45,222.00	1.0
*Jan. 1, 1954—Dec. 31, 1954	127,033.07	1.5
Jan. 1, 1955—June 30, 1955	60,515.70	1.3
Jan. 1, 1956—Dec. 31, 1956	132,513.29	1.3
Jan. 1, 1957—Dec. 31, 1957	179,126.31	1.4
Jan. 1, 1958—June 30, 1958	92,256.65	1.4
Jan. 1, 1959—Dec. 31, 1959	108,614.31	1.1
#Jan. 1, 1960—Dec. 31, 1960	64,547.45	0.6
#Jan. 1, 1961—Dec. 31, 1961	61,219.16	0.5

Source: *Reports of Board of International Trustees and International Secretary-Treasurer, UAW*
* Indicates year in which separate accounts were maintained for engineering and office expenditures. These items appear here as a combined total.
# In 1960 the UAW's organizing function was reorganized. Until the formation of the Technical-Office-Professional Department in 1962 some white-collar expenses were included under the National Organizing Department.

area, a number of limitations should be pointed out. In several instances, only six-months periods were available for comparison. Over time, a considerable portion of the dollar increase shown was absorbed by the higher cost of services purchased by the Union. During this period the Bureau of Labor Statistics Consumer Price Index went from 102.3 in 1948 to 126.5 in 1960 (1947–49 equals 100).[20]

However, as Table 5–1 demonstrates, Office and Technical Department expenditures showed a slow, uneven increase as a

[20] See U.S. Bureau of Labor Statistics, *Consumer Prices in the United States, 1953–1958,* Bulletin no. 1256 (Washington, D.C., 1959), pp. 40–41. Also see *Monthly Labor Review,* February, 1961, p. 125.

percentage of the amount spent for all departmental activities from 1947 to 1954. Something of a plateau developed between 1954 and 1959.

It might also be noted that the Union's general organizing expenditures were from five to ten times as large as all Office and Technical spending between 1947 and 1959.

What Is an Adequate Effort?

There is no completely satisfactory method of evaluating the level of UAW spending for direct office- and technical-worker purposes against some standard of a "proper" proportion of effort. White-collar membership has tended to approximate 5 percent of total UAW membership in the 1950's and early 1960's. In comparison, the average share of the Office and Technical Department (later TOP) in total departmental expenditures has been a little less than 1 percent of all such spending.

However, the activities of the various other administrative departments of the International Union also benefit white-collar members frequently. For example, the activities of the Chrysler Department, the National Aerospace Department, the Agricultural Implement Department, the Research Department, and a number of the other staffs afford direct or indirect service to white-collar as well as to other members.

On the other hand, it is fair to point out a significant anomaly. In the 1950's the Union became increasingly aware that its future influence might be determined by its ability to meet the underlying drift in the composition of the labor force. Yet white-collar expenditures showed no major uptrend between 1954 and 1959. Certainly, in relation to the magnitude of the problem, 1–1.5 percent of total departmental spending was a highly conservative allocation.

In view of the generally unfavorable organizing climate and the Union's inadequate white-collar organizing techniques in those years, mere increased spending for organizing would have resulted in waste and disillusionments. But many years were lost during that decade which might have been devoted to basic white-collar research, experimentation, and pilot organizing attempts. In 1972 such research was still largely lacking.

Because of budgetary limitations and lack of leadership interest the Union was able to do little more than a minimal job of meeting the needs of existing white-collar units. Over the initial twenty-year period the UAW failed to develop a bargaining program of unique interest to white-collar workers. Organizing techniques and publications aimed at office and technical employees were only slightly modified versions of those used with production workers.

Interviews with active white-collar unionists before 1961 showed a strong emphasis upon the International Union's mistakes in assigning blue-collar organizers and servicing representatives to white-collar situations. These staff members frequently used shop language and approaches and had only limited familiarity with white-collar problems.

Interviews with management representatives in the period before the TOP Department's formation directly corroborated this evaluation. They observed that International Union staff members with whom they dealt predominantly applied shop bargaining techniques in the white-collar area.

Staff and Status Quo

In any white-collar organizing situation there is an intricate mixture of social and psychological factors playing within the economic context. Thus the selection of appropriate staff personnel assumes tremendous importance. For too much of the UAW's thirty-year experience with white-collar workers this requirement was largely neglected. This is one of the most difficult factors to resolve within the industrial union framework, for staff positions are inherently political in nature, and the predominant political power resides with the blue-collar group.

The residue of this political process was often apparent in my interviews with UAW staff members in 1959–61. There were certain typical limitations. One of the most important of these was a positive union asset in other contexts: the staff's commit-ment to the traditional principles of industrial unionism. This commitment emphasized working-class solidarity; however, its inherent rejection of status and prestige considerations tended to limit flexibility of thought and imagination in meeting the white-collar problem. These principles were deeply ingrained, not only as beliefs but also as attitudes. In some cases there was the implication of contempt (or at least derision) for white-collar employees by staff members.

At that time there seemed to be considerable staff apathy to-ward the white-collar dilemma as well. Intense concern of the type that is indispensible to necessary, but uncomfortable, changes in the Union and its procedures was not apparent.

On two potentially exploitable issues the prevailing attitude of the staff members interviewed was entirely negative. Seniority was held to be the only workable criterion for regulating advance-ment. "Professionalism" was seen essentially as a management-created myth. It was not envisioned as a possible rallying point for union recruitment of engineers and technicians.

An Unused Resource

For the most part the Union before 1961 grossly neglected a major potential asset. This was the bloc of white-collar members which it had historically accumulated.

The weaknesses here revolved around four points. First, ad-ministrative arrangements for joining white-collar units to the body of the Union were chaotic. In the past some groups were set up as independent white-collar local unions. Some were put into amalgamated white-collar local unions. Some were estab-lished as autonomous units within production local unions, or they were placed within amalgamated production-worker local un-ions. A considerable number were simply lumped into produc-tion-worker units without any structure for maintaining a clear identity or for exercising influence in matters of special concern to themselves.

As a result white-collar workers were often isolated. Their

units were therefore much less effective agents of their members' interests than they might otherwise have been. The International Union was unable to accurately number, communicate with, or judge the trends affecting this potentially important nucleus of members.

Second, white-collar local units lacked any type of council structure that would have permitted adequate communication, coordination, and pursuit of their common interests until after 1963.

Third, the International Union and its leadership appeared to be more in conflict or at cross purposes with white-collar local union leadership than engaged in a mutual effort to solve the white-collar problem. Admittedly, the International officers had to restrain the white-collar local union leaders' sometimes unrealistic enthusiasm for a massive white-collar organizing effort. But this restraint seemed to be dictated more by inertia and indecisiveness than by the proper requirements of caution.

Fourth, except for sporadic attempts the International Union before 1961 had not consistently sought to focus or constructively use the strong interest and competence of white-collar local union officers and active members for organizing purposes.

A Lack of White-Collar Publications

As we have noted in discussing the interview materials concerning unorganized white-collar workers, one of the key channels of approach is through appropriate union publications. Yet, after some twenty years of contact with this group, the UAW had hardly progressed beyond the level of a few white-collar local union newspapers. The special publications needs of white-collar employees were essentially ignored.

The International's newspaper, *Solidarity* (formerly the *United Automobile Worker*), was long of mediocre journalistic quality. It had carried only a limited amount of news oriented to white-collar members and potential members. Even today it seems to be doing much less than it could to improve mutual understanding between white- and blue-collar members of the Union.

Interviews with active white-collar unionists before 1961 demonstrated a strongly critical evaluation of *Solidarity*'s effectiveness with white-collar constituents. Generally it was judged to be less interesting or useful than local union publications, and it was often ignored by white-collar members. Its "blasting" tactics were seen as not effective with these members, and it was felt to be "biased and full of propaganda" by a significant fraction. Only one-fifth of interviewees found it to be "interesting and informative."

This portion of the survey sample was composed of active white-collar union members with a strong involvement in union affairs and with considerable personal identification with labor movement philosophy and goals. It thus seems a major UAW weakness that its main organ of communication with both present and potential white-collar members was regarded as so ineffective.

In other areas of the Union's public relations efforts white-collar criteria were more nearly met. However, a prominent part of the UAW's public relations apparatus, news commentator Guy Nunn, had aimed his presentation largely at the interests of the blue-collar factory worker. For many years the Union seemed unaware of the effects of his caustic partisanship upon the critical ear of the white-collar workers in his audience.

White-Collar Education? Research?

Deservedly famed for some of its innovations in the area of worker education, the UAW singularly failed to use its educational skills as an asset in white-collar organizing.[21] There was

[21] Solomon Barkin, formerly director of research for the Textile Workers' Union, has commented upon the tremendous gap between industry's sophisticated application of social science in personnel management techniques and the unions' reliance upon "time tested" commonsense and traditional methods. See his *Decline of the Labor Movement* (Santa Barbara, Calif.: Center for the Study of Democratic Institutions, 1961), pp. 18–19, 59–60. Communications Workers' President Joseph Beirne has likewise suggested that American unions have sought to meet the pressing problems of the present and future with "the slogans of the past." See his *New Horizons for American Labor* (Washington, D.C.: Public Affairs Press, 1962), p. 160. Both observations applied to the UAW's pre-1961 white-collar organizing and servicing efforts.

little worthwhile collaboration between the Education Department and the Office and Technical Department. Even after the TOP Department reorganization, efforts of the Education Department toward developing a program specifically for the white-collar group appeared extremely limited and tentative.

Nowhere may union research's traditional limitation to short-range problems be more costly to the industrial union's future than in its neglect of the white-collar dilemma. This lack of long-range perspective (and lack of requisite funds and manpower) has meant that little or no important gains in general union understanding of the white-collar problem have been contributed by systematic union research and investigation.

Some Basic Causes of UAW Deficiencies

Up to this point we have attempted to specifically identify some of the shortcomings of the Union in its white-collar efforts. Despite the risk of oversimplification, it may be useful to try to analyze the large-scale causes of these immediate weaknesses before 1961.

An initial area of mistaken policy was the UAW's early willingness to negotiate contract clauses that excluded white-collar workers from organizing drives. Various concessions for blue-collar groups were gained in exchange. The Union was also involved in even more specific exchanges of white-collar interests for blue-collar benefits. Actually or nearly organized office and technical groups were bargained out of existence, as documented above.

UAW Inertia

Several observations help to explain these limited early efforts. A strong ideology of industrial unionism was sometimes dysfunctional. It prevented the Union from taking the necessary fresh look at the white-collar problem and the institutional modification which it demanded. The extremely rapid growth of the Union in its early years minimized the impact of the underlying white-collar trend in the industries under UAW jurisdiction. This was the time when initial experimentation and research might well have been undertaken. Early success at Chrysler probably created a certain overconfidence in the Union's white-collar organizing ability. The massive weight of the blue-collar majority in the Union eliminated any need for political concern by the UAW's officers. Agitation for attention by white-collar local union people was also rather weak until after 1961. White-collar units were thus successfully placed in cold storage. In the 1940's, when white-collar workers were most receptive to organization, the attention of the leadership was preoccupied with the internal factional fight over Communist influence within the UAW and the CIO. With institutional aging, political groupings crystallized and nearly inevitable bureaucratic rigidities developed in the Union. Thus the necessary flexibility for successful adaptation became more difficult to achieve. Political patronage in the organizing departments meant hamstringing of Union efforts because of the "trained incapacity" of blue-collar organizers.

Austerity

By 1957 the Union had become convinced of the importance of white-collar organizing. But now the dues-income sun was no longer shining, so again the leaky roof did not receive adequate attention. Austerity became the order of the day—not new and speculative ventures requiring funds and added manpower.

At the same time the UAW became concerned with the impact of automation upon its blue-collar membership. It committed itself to using its bargaining power in the direction of job security—essentially a defensive reaction—rather than for more aggressive programs.[22]

Finally, the UAW's top officers may have been so involved in community participation that they were literally too busy to

[22] In the words of President Walter Reuther: "We have concluded that the most important problem we have to work on is the question of achieving job security and job opportunity for our members." See UAW, *Proceedings, Special Collective Bargaining Convention, Detroit, Mich.*, April 27–29, 1961, p. 14.

exercise the kind of imaginative leadership within the Union which was necessary to meet the problem at hand. The typical union tendency toward chronic understaffing and overextension of its programs is exemplified in its most extreme form in the UAW.

Origins of Rank-and-File Protest

The ultimate impact of these deficiencies and the obviously crucial need for improvement produced intense frustration among UAW white-collar leaders. This discontent became the basis upon which white-collar units could cooperate politically toward common ends. In 1961 the hour was indeed late.

UAW white-collar election victories between 1957 and 1961 gained a total of 915 potential members in 31 units.[23] In April, 1962, UAW engineering Local 412 pointed out that "Many corporations as a result of their decentralization and modernization programs are eroding our bargaining units at a faster rate than we have been organizing members."[24]

[23] See *White-Collar Report,* no. 205, February 6, 1961, p. B-4, and no. 259, February 22, 1962, p. B-3.
[24] Cited from "Resolution, Organizing the Unorganized," *UAW Local 412 Engineering Leader,* April 25, 1962, p. 10.

Internal Adaptations:
ETO and TOP

6

Assuming that any organization can positively influence its own destiny—a concept of active adaptation rather than of passive, bureaucratic determinism—two alternatives can be discerned in relation to the white-collar problem. A union can attempt to improve *external* factors affecting organizing—for example, through legislation enabling public employees to bargain collectively, as in the Michigan Employment Relations Act of 1965. It can encourage and assist the organizing and bargaining activities of labor-affiliated teacher unions such as the Detroit teachers and the American Federation of Teachers. Ultimately, the union can seek to influence changes in federal legislation which will encourage the unionization of supervisory employees.[1]

A second alternative is to improve the efficiency of the union's organizing instruments and stance from *within* the union itself. Most of the improved performance of the UAW in the white-collar field since 1961 is the result of specific internal changes, although the external organizing context has also concurrently improved. By demonstrating its ability to make these necessary adaptations, the UAW has thus given a qualified "yes" to the question of whether industrial unions can successfully meet the white-collar drift. Industrial unions can continue—and perhaps expand—their influence in the long run, possibly even speeding

[1] See, for example, George Odiorne, "Speech to Meeting of the American Bankers Association," in *White-Collar Report*, no. 503, October 27, 1966, p. C-1.

the present spread of white-collar unionization throughout the economy. For these internal elements are obviously much more within each individual union's control than are the more elusive and more generally determined elements of organizing "climate."

The Continuing Challenge

Pursuing the line of reasoning which UAW Vice-President Leonard Woodcock presented in the 1957 constitutional convention debate described above, an administrative letter of the Union again emphasized in April, 1967, that

> the American labor movement can continue to ignore [the increasing preponderance of white-collar workers in the work force] only at great peril and loss of influence, not only at the bargaining table, but more importantly, in the broad areas of our national life where economic and social problems must be solved and community and national responsibilities must be met.[2]

As a response to this challenge, the UAW's improved performance in white-collar organizing is a classic instance of an adaptive process initiated by a rank-and-file movement. It is probably one of the first by white-collar workers within an industrial union. In 1966 there were indications that a similar development might be under way within the Steelworkers' union.[3]

Robert Cooney, editor of the *AFL-CIO American Federationist,* has stressed the fact that "a key factor consistently underestimated is indigenous leadership and a rank-and-file willingness

[2] Irving Bluestone, administrative assistant to UAW President Walter Reuther, has stated that, unless the growing white-collar work force was substantially organized within the following ten years, "working people will have lost the opportunity to influence social, economic, and legislative decisions." *White-Collar Report,* no. 316, March 28, 1963, p. A-2. Also see no. 529, April 27, 1967, p. A-1.

[3] "The 'revolt' of the white-collar delegates—reminiscent of a similar rank-and-file uprising that led to the Auto Workers' revamping of their white-collar program four years ago—came during floor debate on the Steelworkers' new bargaining program." See *White-Collar Report,* no. 498, September 22, 1966, pp. A-4 to A-5.

to act."[4] UAW experience confirms this observation. An important facilitating element has been the relatively democratic tradition and pattern of the Union's internal political life.[5] In this context, the emergence of an effective rank-and-file white-collar leadership and organization was the outgrowth of the accumulating frustrations examined in the preceding chapter.

It is vital to note that both this rank-and-file movement and its subsequent result, the reorganization and renovation of the UAW's entire white-collar function, are *qualitative* factors. The typical industrial union's problem with white-collar organizing will not yield to merely quantitative measures, no matter how massive. The lack of union success in the past could not have been—nor will it be—remedied simply by spending more money on white-collar organizing, although funds are indispensable in extending the union's reach once basically required changes are made.

Thus an isolated consideration of the monetary budget devoted to white-collar activities would be of only limited value in explaining any new direction of a union or in predicting potential results.

Rejuvenation: The Role of Rank-and-File White-Collar Union Members, 1959–62

It is difficult to find evidence of effective participation by white-collar members in the life of the International Union until after the 1962 convention. Before that, white-collar members had been intermittently hopeful and despairing of stronger action by the UAW leadership in meeting the organizing challenge.

Two events after the 1959 convention were indications of a meaningful change in the nature of white-collar participation; the first of these—the initial instance of regional and national self-organization by the UAW's white-collar members—is the more important. However, the candidacy of a white-collar local

[4] Cited in "Loosening the White Collar," *AFL-CIO American Federationist,* July, 1967, p. 23.

[5] See Jack Stieber, *Governing the UAW* (New York: John Wiley and Sons, 1962), pp. 158–170.

union officer for one of the top policy-making offices of the International Union was also symbolically indicative of a change in white-collar thinking.

The Formation of ETO

Between the 1959 constitutional convention and the 1961 special collective bargaining convention of the UAW, white-collar discontent began to crystallize into a program and an organization. The relative inaction of the International Union's leadership in white-collar affairs can be credited with the development of these innovations by the white-collar rank-and-file.

Shortly before the 1961 special convention, a meeting of Detroit-area white-collar local unions and units at Chrysler and General Motors, along with other interested groups (notably Local 245, Skilled Trades, at Ford), formed the Engineering-Technical-Office Detroit Area Caucus (ETO). The caucus included Local 412 at Chrysler, Local 160 at General Motors, and Local 245 at Ford. Local 1284 at Chrysler and Local 931 at Ford also joined, as did Local 889 and Local 212 (both Chrysler units), soon after the initial organization. Their immediate aim was to strengthen their position in the year's auto negotiations. The long-range goal was "promoting organization and assistance to white-collar workers."[6]

At the special convention they were effective in staging a demonstration supporting a proposal to "Convert Hourly to Salary"—that is, to achieve salaried status for all hourly employees of the industry. The office workers were less optimistic about the job security implications of such a proposal, but they remained within the organization.[7]

The ETO in 1962

After the 1961 convention ETO stimulated the interest of the International Union in calling a national white-collar con-

---

[6] *White-Collar Report,* no. 219, May 15, 1961, pp. A-6 to A-7.
[7] UAW, *Proceedings, Special Collective Bargaining Convention, Detroit, Mich.,* April 27–29, 1961, p. 122.

ference. In earlier years this had been done occasionally, but a number of years had elapsed since the last such meeting. Following this conference Local 412 took the initiative in establishing "better lines of communication between locals with a community of interest in the engineering, technical and office fields."[8]

With the ETO as the organizing center the white-collar group engaged in substantial preparation for the 1962 constitutional convention. Efforts were particularly directed toward obtaining a new and vastly expanded white-collar department within the International Union's administrative structure.

At the convention itself the ETO's immediate objective was not secured; nevertheless, the group felt that substantial gains were achieved. It also appears that the basis for the extension of ETO to a national level was established. The Bureau of National Affairs' *White-Collar Report* stated that the group had gained "active participation and financial support from 15 major white-collar locals in all parts of the country." It was the publication's evaluation that, "While the Caucus has no official status in the UAW International, it appears to be developing an influential voice in white-collar policy matters."[9]

The ETO demonstrated to both blue-collar delegates and to the International Union's leadership that it was capable, well organized, and responsible. It engaged in extensive lobbying for white-collar objectives and prepared and distributed a persuasive statement of the needs of the Union in the white-collar area. The delegates' attention was especially called to the UAW's poor white-collar organizing record in 1960 and 1961. It also contrasted the UAW's eleven petitions for such elections with the Teamsters' eighty-five elections. Not only that, but "the UAW won only 3% of the workers involved in their elections while the Teamsters won nearly 50% of the workers involved in theirs."[10]

[8] See "Letter to All Delegates Attending UAW White-Collar Conference," (Detroit: UAW Local 412, February 22, 1962), p. 1.

[9] *White-Collar Report,* no. 271, May 17, 1962, p. A-9.

[10] See "Organize the Unorganized" (Detroit: Engineering-Technical-Office Detroit Area Caucus, c/o UAW Local 412).

The ETO carefully phrased its aims in terms as nonpolitical as possible. Its leaders maintained that they were not seeking union office but solely the implementation of a program adequate to the dimensions of the white-collar challenge to the UAW. Obviously, such a program must have political implications, and it must be pursued by political methods. However, the ETO's "middle way" successfully minimized opposition to its proposals.

The ETO represented the culmination of a long, slow, and painful political education of the white-collar group within the Union. It signified the establishment of a continuing organized white-collar voice capable of advocating a better UAW response to the white-collar problem.

Inherently, it exemplified the critical role of leadership in institutional adaptation. The ETO was fortunate in having responsible leadership that recognized the hazards of such rank-and-file action. Its leaders were willing both to "needle" the International officers to promote white-collar organization and to participate cooperatively with the International Union in common efforts. Its president, Ray Sullivan, put the alternatives well. "Wild-eyed splinter groups irritate and antagonize. Pacific social organizations are weak and ineffectual."[11]

A White-Collar Campaign

A more direct confrontation of the International Union's leadership on the white-collar issue appeared with the candidacy of office-clerical Local 889's President Wallace Webber for the office of regional co-director. Success here would have meant the placing of a white-collar worker directly at the seat of union power: membership on the executive board of the International Union.

Such a direct political approach had possible advantages and disadvantages for the white-collar bloc. If successful, the candidacy could have meant an importantly increased voice for the white-collar viewpoint in the key decision-making functions of

[11] Ray Sullivan, "President's Column," *UAW Local 412 Engineering Leader,* May 31, 1962, pp. 1, 2.

the board. It definitely dramatized and publicized the presence of white-collar workers within the Union, and it demonstrated the interest of white-collar members in exercising full citizenship and participation within the organization.

On the other hand, white-collar candidacy for office could, conceivably, have led to an exploitation of latent blue-collar resentment by supporters of the incumbent candidates. Thus a greater gap between the blue- and white-collar groups would have been opened. In terms of the central interest of the ETO in obtaining a new white-collar department, the candidacy could have complicated this task considerably. It also seemed that the effort was far too early to be successful.

Whatever the complex of factors operating, the results were a decisive defeat for the white-collar contender. Incumbent Kenneth Morris received 1,151,993 votes. Incumbent George Merrelli received 1,086,694 votes. The white-collar candidate received 69,299 votes.[12]

Effects of the Campaign

The candidacy might easily have embarrassed the ETO by raising doubts about the sincerity of its "nonpolitical" approach. In actuality, it appears that the two activities were essentially independent of each other. By accident, rather than design, the two efforts may have actually complemented each other. It may well be that the incumbent Reuther group's response to the campaign was to grant greater concessions to the ETO than might otherwise have been the case.

Following the convention ETO leaders met at length with the International executive board and were jointly involved in planning some fundamental changes in the Union's white-collar policies and structure.

The new director of the subsequently renovated white-collar department later reported:

[12] See UAW, *Proceedings, 18th Constitutional Convention, Atlantic City, N.J.,* May 4–10, 1962, p. 794.

For a period of many weeks, conferences and personal discussions were held in an effort to review every aspect of this elusive subject. Talks were held with officers and members of white-collar local unions, searching for their ideas, their complaints and their suggestions.

Many hours were spent discussing the many facets of this task with the leadership of other unions, with UAW regional directors and their staffs.

After analyzing the results of this intensive sampling, several recommendations were proposed to the International Executive Board and approval was granted. . . .[13]

A number of significant changes ensued. The former Office and Technical Department was renamed the Technical, Office, and Professional Department—TOP Department. The importance of intangibles was well illustrated here. The name became a useful status symbol. And it lent itself to effective use as a special insignia for letter-heads, authorization cards, organizing literature, and other promotional material. As the director pointed out in his report to the 1964 Convention, "While, to some, this might appear to be a minor development, the new name has created considerable interest and attention and is proving quite valuable in our organizing effort."[14]

A fundamentally "important and very strategic weapon" for organizing resulted from the executive board's approval of permitting newly organized white-collar groups the right of self-determination in deciding the nature of their local affiliation or structure. "Under this new policy, these groups are now permitted to make their own democratic choice of three alternatives: formation of their own local union, affiliation with the production and maintenance local at their plant, or affiliation with an amalgamated white-collar group in the area."[15] Director Fraser

[13] UAW, *Report of President Walter P. Reuther to the 19th Constitutional Convention, Atlantic City, N.J.,* March 20–27, 1964, Part III, Departmental Reports, p. 177.
[14] *Ibid.*
[15] *Ibid.*

acknowledged that this freedom of choice had proved "exceedingly helpful" in voiding an argument that had been used quite successfully in management's anti-organizing efforts in the past.

The primary responsibility for white-collar organizing was explicitly delegated to the new department's director. He acknowledged the indispensable role of the ETO and its leaders in initiating changes in the UAW's white-collar functions at the founding meeting of the Michigan White-Collar Advisory Council. He also confirmed earlier portions of the historical analysis above in these words: "Quite obvious to us was the fact that there existed a complete lack of communication between the International Union and our white-collar groups. In many cases, especially with the smaller groups, they felt they were being overlooked and were unable to keep abreast of current developments."[16]

Sine Qua Non: **Leadership**

Following the structural renovation of the International Union's white-collar section, much of the ETO leadership group was co-opted into full-time staff positions with the TOP Department.

If any single factor can be looked on as indispensable to the process of adaptation to new circumstances in the environment of a union, it is that of leadership. This points up one of the prime faults of the usual, static view of bureaucratic functioning. It neglects or assumes that leadership is essentially a passive, dependent variable.

In the UAW, as a case in point, quality leadership has made a tremendous difference in the Union's potential in the white-collar field.

The initial rank-and-file action originated with concerned, effective local union leaders. This concern was translated into an organization and a program within the quite permissive limits of political process in the Autoworkers' union. In response, the International Union leadership gave white-collar organizing responsibility to a highly vigorous, enterprising, flexible, and

---

[16] *White-Collar Report,* no. 341, September 19, 1962, p. C-2.

aspiring new member of the executive board. The new director had the personal insight and capability to work jointly with the indigenous white-collar leadership to establish a much more effective structure, to improve communications in both directions, to recruit highly competent organizers and staff from among local union leaders, and to introduce improved organizing literature and techniques.

It is important to note that many of these changes were developed and advocated to the International Union by Local 889 as early as January, 1960. Yet implementation waited upon the political coalescence of the white-collar group and upon the impact of ETO and the Webber candidacy.[17]

The payoff of the developments which we are tracing can be somewhat superficially measured by improved election statistics and membership gains. Fundamentally, however, the more important result has been the *qualitative* upgrading of the Union's white-collar functioning as a whole.

An additional gain in the internal position of the white-collar group occurred in 1964 with the elevation of a woman member, Olga Madar, to executive board membership. Interestingly, her political supporters at the convention argued that "organizing in the all-important white-collar field means organizing WOMEN!"[18]

The new board member was subsequently given responsibility for the Servicing Division of the TOP Department.[19] This resulted in a useful division of functions and aided the effectiveness of the department's organizing efforts as well. At the same time, this meant—in some sense—a doubling of white-collar "representation" in the key policy-making board of the total union.

To sum up: throughout my years of contact with the UAW white-collar leadership, I have been singularly impressed by the intelligence, dedication, and concern of the white-collar local

[17] Wallace Webber et al., "Analysis of the White-Collar Organizational Problem: Presentation before the UAW International Executive Board" (Detroit: UAW Local 889, January 20, 1960).

[18] *White-Collar Report,* no. 365, March 5, 1964, p. A-4.

[19] See "Women of Eastern Salute: Olga M. Madar," *Eastern Michigan University Alumni Magazine,* January, 1967, p. 5, for a brief summary of the new board member's extensive activities in union and community affairs.

union people. In that period many have moved into vital positions in the International Union structure. The changes described
are, at bottom, a remarkable testimony of the impact of individual competence upon the functioning of a bureaucratic structure of great extent and operational scope.

White-Collar Publications

To help fill the communications gap, in 1963 the new TOP
Department initiated publication of the *TOP Reporter*—a concise but effective newsletter issued about eight times a year.
This added a note of professional, white-collar visibility and
provided a channel for news on organizing, National Labor Relations Board rulings, arbitration awards, local union activities,
reports on white-collar conferences, pictures of local and International Union officers, and news of relevant national events,
such as teacher organization. According to the director, the
mailing list included staff representatives, local union leadership,
"and many unorganized groups."[20]

White-Collar Structure

At several points in preceding chapters I have noted the UAW's
underutilization, before 1961, of the resources represented in its
bloc of historically accumulated white-collar membership. The
lack of communication cited above, and the isolation of many
white-collar units attached to production locals even in the
Detroit area, were also apparent in earlier interviews.

In light of this problem, the formation of advisory councils
on the initiative of the International Union—beginning with the
Eastern Advisory Council in 1963—was a major gain for rationalization of the relationships between white-collar units and
the International Union through the TOP Department.

Five regional white-collar councils were established: Eastern,
Michigan, Mid-Western, Western, and Canadian. An overall

[20] UAW, *Report of President Walter P. Reuther to the 19th Constitutional
Convention*, p. 179.

coordinating council was structured to include representatives from the regional councils. This became the International Advisory Council by December, 1964.

In terms of maximum white-collar effectiveness, the advisory councils seemed well named. If, as the new director suggested, they are actively used in the future for "local union leadership to give practical advice regarding our activities in the white-collar area," then the councils should prove to be a permanent asset. Here the long prior experience of the UAW with somewhat similar blue-collar councils, if adapted to white-collar differences, can confer valuable organizational benefits.[21]

The 1966 convention evaluated the council structure as extremely valuable in providing identification for white-collar groups and in promoting communication. They constituted a forum for analysis and discussion of the many complex problems of white-collar workers. The convention emphasized that it was necessary and desirable to continue to strengthen the councils.[22]

Advisory Council Conference

In cooperation with the advisory councils, the TOP Department convened an international collective bargaining conference in Detroit in March, 1967, as a prelude to the year's automobile negotiations. Executive board member and TOP Department Servicing Director Olga Madar indicated that the conference was a "highly significant event" for technical, office, and professional members. Bargaining resolutions for consideration of the Union's special collective bargaining convention were formulated in a unique panel format which dealt separately with issues such as unit erosion, attrition, retraining, and stock and profit-sharing plans, as well as more traditional bargaining concerns. Top officers of the International Union, including President Walter Reuther and Secretary-Treasurer Emil Mazey, spoke to the

[21] "Statements to Autoworkers' Michigan White-Collar Advisory Council by Douglas Fraser, UAW Technical, Office, and Professional Director," *White-Collar Report,* no. 341, September 19, 1963, p. C-1.

[22] UAW, *Proceedings, 20th Constitutional Convention, Long Beach, Calif.,* May 16–21, 1966, p. 75.

delegates. Four of the Union's regional directors were also guests.[23]

Thus the council structure has tremendous "policy projecting ability," as Director Fraser has suggested. It offers a means of formulating policy recommendations and of mobilizing the necessary political strength of the white-collar bloc to support those recommendations within the total union. However, it does not now appear that this potential has yet been entirely realized or that leadership within the councils has regained the initiative exercised by the ETO in 1961–62.

Organizing Gains

Table 6–1 gives a useful measure of the changed outlook for white-collar organizing by the UAW. The "turnaround" in the organizing trend is essentially coincident with the changes in leadership, structure, and techniques which have been examined. There appears to be a definite causal relationship between these changes and improved white-collar performance by the Union.

In the years since the TOP Department was reorganized there has been a general improvement in organizing performance. A larger number of organizing campaigns have been carried through the election stage, the won/lost average has been stable or improving despite the greater activity (a point of union pride that unfortunately exerts an inhibiting influence in reaching for "doubtful" organizing opportunities), and the number of eligible new members gained has increased substantially. The latter measure is, for our purposes, the most significant one.

The favorable trend in these figures during the 1960's was, from the standpoint of the Union, clearly in the right direction. But the small absolute size of these statistics immediately raises the question of increased expenditures for staff and resources to

[23] See Olga M. Madar, "Letter to Officers and Delegates of the T.O.P. Advisory Councils" (Detroit: UAW Technical, Office, Professional Department, March 24, 1967). Also see Phyllis Burgin, "Minutes of the First Annual T.O.P. International Conference" (Detroit: UAW Technical, Office, Professional Department, March 22, 1967).

TABLE 6–1. UAW PARTICIPATION IN NATIONAL LABOR RELATIONS BOARD ELECTIONS INVOLVING WHITE-COLLAR EMPLOYEES

	Elections			*UAW Rank*		
Year	*Won*	*Lost*	*Eligible New Members Gained*	*By Elections Won*	*By Eligible Members Gained*	*Total Organized (All Unions)*
1957	13	10	550	2	3	5,700
1958	6	7	220	4	6	3,900
1959	6	3	130	4	7	3,660
1960	4	10	45	4	11	3,005
1961	2	11	20	7	19	4,660
1962	6	9	300	10	6	5,880
1963	15	14	550	4	4	6,495
1964	14	14	490	4	4	6,780
1965	24	13	1,305	3	2	7,605
1966	27	24	1,145	3	2	9,085
1967	29	12	1,315	5	4	15,090
1968	24	19	1,315	5	3	11,175
1969	27	20	785	3	3	10,695
1970	31	16	815	2	4	11,110
1971	30	20	1,300	2	2	12,085

NOTE: This summary covers primarily industrial white-collar employees.
SOURCE: White-Collar Report, Nos. 47, 99, 150, 205, 259, 311, 364, 417, 472, 521, 565, 577, 733, 786.

take advantage of the organizing possibilities which these trends suggest.

Organizing Approaches

The newly organized TOP Department initially gave substantial attention to the process of automation and its apparent implications for office and technical employees. Automation was a major theme of the founding conference of the Michigan TOP Advisory Council and provided an important focus for discussion.

However, aside from locally favorable, unsettled situations which offer an occasional union opportunity in individual automation installations, it seems very doubtful whether automation.

in its present form, offers any important, exploitable issue for organizing purposes. Careful company attention to the displacement aspects and the systematic use of transfer and attrition tend to quiet employee fears. As often pointed out, "the man not hired" is beyond the union's reach.

The automation possibility seems to illustrate a frequent mistake of unions seeking white-collar members. There is a continuing wistful hope that some single, overriding issue or organizing appeal can be discovered which will prove the magic key to success with these workers. Barring some unforeseen, dramatic event in the economic, social, or political order, it seems likely that there simply *is* no such unique issue or appeal.

Rather than implying that white-collar workers cannot be organized, this really means that organizing becomes a situation-by-situation, local-issue-after-local-issue task—a task to be met by a combination of increasingly skilled, mechanically competent organizing personnel, a constant union readiness to identify and move into favorable openings, and an evolving set of improved organizing techniques.

The Key: Personnel

As Barkin has suggested, union organizing is usually a neglected and low-status function within mature unions.[24] This pattern constitutes a major handicap in the white-collar field. The organizer, to an unorganized white-collar group, *is* the union. His manner, language, dress, and total personality provide the most concrete clues which the group can examine to determine the union's ability to understand and meet special white-collar needs and to offset the negative stereotypes held by a sizable number of white-collar workers.

The TOP Department, once organized, moved rapidly to deal with this requirement. Many of the active agents in the ETO movement were employed by the International Union to exercise

---

[24] Solomon Barkin, *Decline of the Labor Movement* (Santa Barbara, Calif.: Center for the Study of Democratic Institutions, 1961), pp. 26–28, 58–60.

basic organizing as well as administrative responsibilities. A perusal of the *TOP Reporter* shows a conscious attempt to give adequate personal credit for organizing victories to the particular staff members directly involved.

At the same time, TOP experimented with the use of supplementary part-time organizers who were employed after hours or brought into particular campaigns "on leave" from their regular white-collar jobs. Aside from the direct assistance rendered, this had the additional dividend of identifying potential talent for permanent upgrading. It also created a base for the substantial expansion of organizing capability if large-scale opportunities should appear.

The part-time group was enthusiastically commended by Director Fraser in his 1964 report as a "valuable adjunct to our regular staff." In 1966 he stated, "Special commendation must go to our trained and competent part-time organizers. Their dedication and efforts are major ingredients in our organizing successes."[25]

It now appears that problems in administration and aspiration for full-time employment have led to a much more limited use of these volunteers. Nevertheless, it does seem that this device can still offer useful service, if a reserve of interested local union members were maintained to provide specialized occupational counsel to the full-time TOP organizers and to work with the regular staff at key junctures in specific campaigns.

The Emphasis on Autonomy

My consistent thesis has been that there is a sense of difference on the part of the white-collar worker which is a matter of pride. An appeal to this pride has been a regular theme of the TOP Department's leadership and publications. Thus, in the director's words, "The UAW recognizes that the problems, motivations and

[25] See UAW, *Report of President Walter P. Reuther to the 19th Constitutional Convention*, p. 178. Also see UAW, *Report of President Walter P. Reuther to the 20th Constitutional Convention, Long Beach, Calif.*, May 16–21, 1966, p. 150.

needs of white-collar workers are different and require different approaches and answers."[26]

The Union's executive board in 1962 approved a recommendation of the TOP Department providing for the "preservation of identity and self-determination on all matters pertinent to their own interest" for newly organized office groups. After deciding the type of local unit affiliation, each unit has the opportunity to enter negotiations on a contract "which gives prime recognition to their own particular problems."[27]

These provisions for white-collar autonomy have since been strongly pointed up in organizing leaflets. Such leaflets have called attention to the fact that the unit's bargaining committee would be white collar and that separate, special attention and service by white-collar staff members were available to new units.[28] The white-collar specialization in the TOP Department structure and in the advisory councils have likewise been cited to prospective members.

The guarantee of individual membership rights provided by the UAW's uniquely constituted Public Review Board has also been judged especially relevant to white-collar attitudes. Its make-up and functions have been publicized in informative detail in organizing campaigns.[29] This appeal system, originated by the Upholsterer's union and strengthened by UAW adoption, has also been adopted by the Teachers' union.

The Corporate Chain

UAW white-collar history demonstrates the tendency for organizing gains to follow along the lines of corporate structure. Following the reorganization in 1962 and 1963 this organizing technique was again emphasized. The Chrysler precedent sug-

[26] "Statements by Douglas Fraser," p. C-4.

[27] *TOP Reporter,* February, 1965, p. 4.

[28] *White-Collar Report,* no. 327, June 13, 1963, pp. C-1 to C-3, gives the text and reproduction of this type of organizing leaflet.

[29] See, for example, the Vertol–Boeing leaflets in *White-Collar Report,* no. 378, June 4, 1964, pp. C-7 and C-8. For an evaluation of the Public Review Board, see Jack Stieber, *Governing the UAW,* pp. 79–83.

gests the ultimate potential of this method in the auto industry. At the founding meeting of the Eastern Advisory Council in 1963, the new director pointed this out in concise terms: "If we are able to break through in General Motors and Ford and hold up an acceptable contract, we will be on our way."[30]

This principle is also visible in the frequency with which TOP election victories occur within the Chrysler Corporation. Apparently white-collar workers in a given company are differentially impressed by the example of fellow employees in other company locations and by the negotiated gains of the organized group.

TOP Department organizing experience has verified that a uniquely favoring situation is produced by corporate mergers. Merger normally threatens the intricate web of personal relationships out of which the unorganized white-collar worker traditionally sought to construct his own "security system" in the absence of formal organization. This source of white-collar unionization was frequently identified by management representatives in my early interviews, as well as by local union leaders and International staff members. A major corporate reorganization produces roughly similar effects.

Insofar as specific industries are undergoing concentration—a general movement in most of the basic industries included in the jurisdiction of industrial unions—there is thus a certain organizing vulnerability implied simply by economic trends. Both the unsettling impact of the merger and the lengthened "chain" that results are union organizing assets.

The Ford Formula

The efficacy of a combination of tandem benefits for white-collar employees, a special concern and attention by an alert personnel department, a thorough supervisory training program, and aggressive, campaign-by-campaign opposition to UAW organizing attempts are at least some of the ingredients which have prevented the TOP Department from penetrating Ford.

[30] *White-Collar Report,* no. 316, March 28, 1963, p. A-2.

By October, 1965, the department was self-confident enough to announce "a nation-wide organizing drive among 30,000 Ford Motor salaried employees."[31] In March, 1966, election petitions were filed for several Ford locations. The Union cited extensive Ford resistance:

> The Ford personnel department has been busily engaged in a "fence-mending" operation, holding individual talks with employees, changing classifications and trying to correct inequities which they feel are sources of agitation. Some reports indicate ten and twenty dollar across the board increases in certain locations, together with a more liberal application of the merit increase program. For the first time, Ford salaried employees are allowed to receive prizes from the Ford Suggestion program. In other areas, management trainees are being recruited from colleges and placed on jobs in prospective bargaining units. The recruits are being paid salaries over those paid to regular employees to give them special inducements to remain aloof from organization.

Not without a certain humor was the final comment: "One committee at the Dearborn Engineering complex reports the supervisors run around picking up leaflets and authorization cards as fast as they pass them out."[32]

In any event, late in 1965 Ford security police ejected union organizers from company property at the Ford central offices in Dearborn. The Union subsequently filed unfair labor practices charges against the company with the National Labor Relations Board, "for the first time since the '30's. . . ."[33]

For this or for tactical reasons, the next visit of UAW white-collar organizers to the central office building took place without incident.

The company was later found guilty of an unfair labor practice involving an incident in which an employee was verbally reprimanded for distributing authorization cards before the start of her working shift. Company attorneys agreed to a settlement

[31] *TOP Reporter,* October, 1965, p. 1.

[32] *Ibid.,* March, 1966, pp. 1, 3.

[33] *UAW Solidarity,* January, 1966, p. 14; *TOP Reporter,* December, 1965, p. 1.

which required Ford to post notices that it would not interfere with, restrain, or coerce the company's employees in the exercise of their right to self-organization. Ford agreed:

> We will not promulgate, maintain, enforce, or apply any rule or regulation prohibiting our employees, when they are on non-working time, from distributing handbills or other literature in behalf of any labor organization in non-working areas of our property. We will not prohibit our employees, during non-working time, from soliciting their fellow employees to join or support the International Union, UAW (AFL-CIO) or any other labor organization.[34]

In the spring of 1966 an NLRB election was held at the Cleveland area Ford stamping plant, as cited above. The vote was close (74 to 62) but against the Union. TOP Department gave credit for the defeat to 21 college co-op students who had been included in the unit and had "campaigned vigorously against the union. . . . Most of the students were recruited from college campuses by Ford talent scouts. . . . It seems clear that one important consideration in their selection is their attitude concerning unionism."[35] The Union maintained that the voting pattern indicated that regular Ford employees voted in favor of UAW representation. The Union at first indicated an interest in seeking a review of the students' status in the election, but soon decided to drop the matter.[36]

In view of the ability of the Union to initiate a series of election gains along corporate lines after a breakthrough, the defeat, although in a small unit, was of vital importance. But the closeness of the vote may indicate a trend, when compared with the 254 to 62 vote against the UAW in the 1947–48 election campaign at the Lincoln-Mercury plant in Dearborn. On the other hand, it should be noted that the Union was rejected in five elections at Ford between 1965 and 1968.[37]

[34] *TOP Reporter,* January, 1966, p. 1.

[35] *Ibid.,* May, 1966, p. 1.

[36] *White-Collar Report,* no. 548, September 7, 1967, pp. A-7 to A-8; no. 549, September 14, 1967, p. A-10.

[37] The five were Metuchen, N.J., Dearborn Proving Ground, Dearborn draftsmen, Nashville glass plant, and Cleveland stamping plant. See *ibid.,* no. 586, May 30, 1968, p. A-7.

In view of the obvious strategic need to organize Ford as a key to the ultimate coverage of most white-collar autoworkers, it is difficult to justify the Union's tentative, intermittent organizing gestures there. The UAW's apparent unwillingness to commit substantial resources to a persisting, corporation-wide drive that would stretch the company's anti-union efforts beyond the point of effective resistance is difficult to explain. This reluctance probably reflects an internal UAW political problem which must be resolved if meaningful, industry-wide organizing is to proceed.

This is the dilemma of every similarly situated industrial union interested in white-collar organization. Can the conservative influence of existing blue-collar–management relations be successfully circumvented to permit the mounting of adequate organizing drives? Perhaps in this sense white-collar unionism in industry waits upon the understanding of blue-collar unionists in the corporate councils and departments of the international unions and the blue-collar local union leadership. Until these secondary leaders are willing to take the inherent risk of at least temporarily jeopardizing existing bargaining relationships with corporate management, it may not be politically possible for the top union leadership to authorize white-collar drives in the major companies. If this hypothesis is correct, it helps to explain the attention given by departments such as TOP to peripheral supplier firms, despite the fact that these would normally "fall in line" if an organizing pattern were once established at the level of the Big Three.

Conceivably, such a pattern might also be initiated by a victory at General Motors. However, the situation there has proved similarly unpromising, as indicated by TOP election losses among plant clerical workers in the Fisher Body Division in Detroit (by 18 to 51 in May, 1967) and among technicians at the General Motors technical center (in April, 1966, with a 66 to 153 "no union" vote).[38]

[38] See, for example, *TOP Reporter,* May, 1966, p. 1, and *White-Collar Report,* no. 530, May 4, 1967, p. A-11. Also note *White-Collar Report,* no. 476, April 21, 1966, p. A-6.

Organizing Strategy and Tactics

To complete this consideration of the changes which have followed the reorganization of the UAW's white-collar functions, it is worthwhile to analyze the evolution of the Department's organizing strategy and tactics.

Before 1961 a rather conservative organizing philosophy governed Office and Technical Department campaigns. An attempt was made to maintain a high ratio of successful elections, even at the cost of lower total organizing gains. As much as 60 percent of the unit was required to have signed cards before filing an election petition. In contrast, unions such as the Office Employees International Union pursued a much more aggressive and risk-taking approach.

Director Fraser pointed out a significant change in this policy in his remarks at the founding of the Michigan Advisory Council. He mentioned the need for seeking elections more quickly and frequently and pointed out that the Union would seek elections if 30 percent of eligible employees would sign authorization cards.[39]

In view of the volatility of issues sufficiently crucial to cause white-collar employees to consider unionization, such a policy seems more promising for the union.

"We'll Be Back"

Another evolving principle of white-collar organizing is under development by the TOP Department. *White-Collar Report* commented upon this pattern of UAW activity when the Union won an election among technical employees at Continental Motors in Muskegon, Michigan, by a 98 to 72 vote. It pointed out that the UAW "was following its practice of returning to the scene of earlier defeats." The Union had won an office unit at that location two years before, but it had been rejected by the technicians: "It was the union's third successful repeat campaign

[39] *White-Collar Report,* no. 341, September 19, 1963, p. A-3.

in the past six months."[40] The other cases cited included Burroughs Corporation and Mueller Brass employees.

This pattern also supports the view that clerical employees are usually somewhat easier to organize than technicians. The later reversal of the technicians' opinion may thus be a result of observing the initial experience of the office units in negotiating and bargaining. Given a second chance at a later date, this favorable evaluation is reflected in a pro-union vote.

As Receiver

In 1957 the UAW suffered a major defeat in the white-collar field when it lost bargaining rights for Minneapolis-Honeywell employees in a decertification election. This election followed the very brief UAW affiliation of the previously independent unit of the company's engineering and technical employees. It is doubtful whether any set of UAW-devised remedies could have avoided the loss at the time. However, this 1957 event may ultimately indicate one of the most productive patterns of white-collar unionization.

The white-collar workers' penchant for independence, combined with provocative employment circumstances, sometimes leads to spontaneous, self-organizing efforts. The resulting organization, which George Strauss calls "a half-way house on the road toward unionism," is usually followed by a period of negotiation and bargaining.[41] Pressures on this inherently isolated and exposed unit ultimately lead to a crisis in which support from a more stable and experienced bargaining agent becomes imperative, or the independent organization dissolves.[42]

In such situations existing industrial unions can, by virtue of their sizable financial resources and experienced staffs, become the beneficiaries of these independent attempts. The premium

[40] *Ibid.,* no. 522, March 9, 1967, p. A-5.
[41] George Strauss, "Professionalism and Occupational Associations," *Industrial Relations,* May, 1963, p. 10.
[42] One of the best studies of the independent union is Arthur B. Shostak's *America's Forgotten Labor Organization* (Princeton: Princeton University Press, 1962).

here is upon the union's alertness and informative contacts in the local area.

Such organizations have been an important source of white-collar members for the UAW—for example, this was true historically of the Society of Designing Engineers. Much more recently this pattern has been exemplified by the affiliation of the Independent Engineers and Draftsmen Association of the Allis-Chalmers Company with the UAW in April, 1965. "The IEDA has a membership in excess of 300 with a potential of over 6,000 eligibles."[43]

In most instances these independents tend to be only partially covering their constituency because of an unwillingness to press for union security agreements. With a change of affiliation the new representative is often in a position to push strongly for full membership, through either recruitment or a union shop provision. Thus the potential membership involved may be much greater than the simple initial transfer of affiliation might indicate.

The potential of independent-to-affiliate is well illustrated by the UAW's securing of a service contract with the Northern Electric Office Employee's Association for nearly 3,000 members. The association was on strike and sought UAW assistance in settling the dispute and in negotiating a new contract with their Montreal employer. The occasion was sufficiently important to occasion a visit by President Walter Reuther to the association's membership meeting.[44]

Five hundred new members were brought into the Association by the terms of the settlement's security agreement. An additional dividend was a vote by over 200 London, Ontario, members of the association to enter the UAW a few months later. The next week more than 100 of Northern Electric's Belleville, Ontario, offices voted to take the same action.[45]

The structure initially established by independent organization paid off similarly for the UAW in late 1967, when 600 clerical

---

[43] *TOP Reporter,* April, 1965, p. 4.
[44] *Ibid.,* July–August, 1967, pp. 1, 3.
[45] *Ibid.,* November–December, 1967, p. 4.

and technical employees included in an independent union at the Leeds and Northrup Company in Philadelphia were certified to the UAW in a successful election contest.[46]

Around the Canadian Flank?

Another promising possibility which the UAW's new white-collar organizing team has been productively exploring is that offered by the decidedly more favorable organizing framework in the province of Ontario.

Representation procedures there are considerably simpler than in the United States. A demonstration of support for unionization through the verification of at least 55 percent of a unit's signed authorization cards is generally adequate for certification.[47]

Here it might be noted that a Windsor local union of white-collar Ford employees has existed successfully for many years, even though Ford in the United States has consistently resisted the UAW. In May, 1965, 180 office employees of the Bramlea Division of Ford Motor Company of Canada were granted "automatic" recognition by the Ontario Labour Board.[48]

Quite conceivably, an expansion of UAW white-collar membership in Canada could directly help to sustain and improve the total white-collar posture and political position within the International Union. Thus it could have a long-run impact upon UAW white-collar organization in the United States. A special boost to organizing might also be imparted to employees in those corporations operating in both jurisdictions—a frequent occurrence in the automobile and agricultural implement industries.

The possible leverage is to be noted in the fact that Canadian Chrysler office workers were able to negotiate participation in a

[46] *Ibid.,* September–October, 1967, p. 1.

[47] For a broad survey of organizing in Canada, see W. Donald Wood, "White-Collar Unionism in Canada, 1967," Outline of presentation made to Shell Canada management course held at Queen's University (Kingston, Ontario) Industrial Relations Centre, June 5–23, 1967.

[48] *TOP Reporter,* May, 1965, p. 3.

stock thrift plan in 1963. This subsequently became a part of the U.S. Chrysler contract settlement in 1964.[49]

Favorable Organizing Situations

To conclude this discussion of white-collar organizing strategy and tactics, it is worthwhile to summarize the general nature of the organizing problem and to identify the types of specific local discontent which lend themselves to exploitation by the union.

The analytical perspective throughout has been that white-collar employees choose unionization when, in a particular employment situation, the union's image becomes sufficiently compatible with their own self-image to be an acceptable option. The organizer's basic role is to reduce the conflict between these two images as much as possible. Part of this involves an alert exploitation of the unique factors in each individual organizing situation that affect the potential member's perception of both images—self and union.

It is impossible to treat all of the possibilities. But it does appear that the TOP Department organizing experience and my interview study suggest typical issues which frequently provide openings for the union.

Thus unions have found white-collar employees to be favorable to organization where abuses of job classification and the maintenance of salary "secrecy" exist. Substandard wages and numerous inequities are likewise useful to the union. Arbitrary discharges, poor supervisory practices, favoritism, and discrimination produce white-collar discontent. Insecurity on the job, over-routinization of work, the "dead-ending" of channels for advancement, and impersonal, mass treatment make for the acceptance of unionism.

The union looks for situations where there is pressure to produce. Layoffs out of line of seniority and the displacement of present employees by key people who "coat-tail in" with shifts in higher management arouse white-collar fears and resentment.

[49] *Ibid.,* December, 1963, pp. 1, 4, and September, 1964, pp. 1, 4.

Company failure to communicate reasons for changes in its practices or policies is costly to white-collar morale. Finally, a lack of merit increases and company inattention to individual grievances bring about organizing openings.[50]

Management's View

Table 6–2, although based on quite a limited number of instances, suggests the ranking of causes of unionization by management representatives with some personal experience in this matter. Fifteen such situations were encountered in my interviews with the management group.

TABLE 6–2. MANAGEMENT'S EXPLANATION OF WHITE-COLLAR UNIONIZATION

Question: How do you explain the union's ability to organize your white-collar workers?

Wage level too low; numerous inequities	33%
Poor handling of white-collar workers by management	33%
Disrupting effects of a merger or reorganization	20%
Desire for job security under a seniority system	20%
Need for a fair classification system and practices	13%
Poor supervision	13%
A crucial grievance, other than a discharge	13%
Reasons not entirely clear, organization came as a surprise to management	13%
Firing of a key person	7%
Favoritism	7%
Closeness to shop union	7%
Group consciousness already existed	7%

In the situations mentioned in Table 6–2 it is important to note that a wide variety of factors are, in management's experience, apparently capable of giving rise to white-collar unionism. Most of these are nonfinancial in nature, although wages are also important.

[50] See Robert J. Shebal, "White-Collar Organizational Issues" (Detroit: Office and Technical Workers Department, International UAW-AFL-CIO, February 2, 1959), pp. 1–15.

White-Collar Bargaining Goals

Although we are primarily concerned with organizing, the white-collar bargaining program which is slowly evolving within the UAW and elsewhere in the economy has a substantial relationship to the acceptability of unionism among white-collar employees. For present members, it is the answer to the question, "What have you done for me—lately?" And for potential members it represents a possible goal and a concrete indication of what the union can hope to obtain for them, once organized.

At this point, the UAW has still not been successful in creating a uniquely attractive white-collar bargaining "package." A major negotiating handicap of UAW white-collar employees in the 1967 negotiations was that the basic settlement achieved at Ford was a blue-collar design—$.20 for production and $.50 for skilled trades. It was only with a great deal of modification and labor that white-collar bargainers were able to translate this to meet the demands of the infinitely more varied and ambiguous shadings of classifications and skills in the office and technical salary structure.

One of the basic arguments for inclusion of white-collar workers in industrial unions is that, while these workers are distinctively different in some respects from blue-collar employees, they have strongly parallel economic needs and interests.

That this argument is valid for the most part is borne out by the bargaining of white-collar units within the UAW. White-collar contracts tend to be modifications of the blue-collar bargaining pattern—but adapted to the special interests and position of the white-collar membership.

Thus the 1964 Chrysler white-collar settlement involved improved pensions, early retirement with pension supplements, medical and hospital insurance, added holidays, increased vacations, increased wages, better supplemental unemployment benefits, and other gains similar to the production and maintenance contract. But there were significant differences as well. These included improvements in the salary grade structure, additional steps in the automatic progression schedule, and the right to participate in the stock-thrift program.[51]

An important white-collar variation involves a recognition of merit factors, particularly in the engineering and technical areas. Thus the negotiated salary grade structure at Chrysler demonstrates a direct correlation between the level of salary and the amount of progression based upon merit.

An additional, but unrealized, 1964 bargaining demand proposed that jobs be reduced only on the basis of attrition. White-collar employees also requested a scholarship program.

Management Benefits

One of the devices often used by companies to combat an interest in unionization among white-collar employees is to include them as members of management in establishing eligibility for certain company-sponsored benefit programs. While frequently effective in the past, the use of this approach by the major unorganized companies may be undergoing reevaluation.

In December, 1966, a group of cost estimators at Chrysler voted for the UAW 123 to 70 in an NLRB election. In subsequent negotiations to include these employees under the existing engineering contract, the Union was successful in securing the retention of the management benefits program for the new members. *White-Collar Report* proclaimed, "UAW Retains 'Management Employee' Benefits in Unprecedented Memorandum of Agreement": "The memorandum declares that these employees who already have benefits above the ones provided in the agreement will retain the same benefits in number and kind."[52] The publication pointed out that the breakthrough in benefits would serve as a wedge for improving contract provisions for all other Chrysler salaried employees in the next negotiations. The benefits in question included a superior life insurance policy, better disability coverage at retirement, a

[51] *TOP Reporter,* September, 1967, p. 2.
[52] See *White-Collar Report,* no. 530, May 4, 1967, p. A-10.

special supplemental unemployment benefits plan, a program for purchasing company cars, promotional increase provisions, and "certain pay policies concerning computation of overtime."

In more general terms, TOP Department policy has evolved into an aggressive, steadfast commitment to resist any withdrawal of benefits by companies from employees following unionization. This has included a willingness to authorize strike action if such an attempt is made. It seems clear that if the union does not take this position, companies inevitably will be tempted to use this possibility as an effective threat during organizing attempts and to cite instances where such losses have occurred.

The evolving bargaining program of the TOP Department and the advisory councils included as an additional future goal a fairly extensive list of demands approved by the special collective bargaining convention of the Union which was held prior to the 1967 negotiations. These covered joint union-employer administration of testing and training programs, promotion of qualified production workers to white-collar jobs, narrowing of the gap between minimum and maximum rates in salary classifications, complete automatic progression in additional classifications, and the elimination of overlapping rates between pay grades.[53] A similarly expansive list of objectives was compiled by UAW white-collar members before the 1970 negotiations; however, the actual gains achieved closely paralleled production and maintenance ones.[54]

TOP's Future

The key question toward which analysis always points is, "What about the future?" To conclude the present chapter it is desirable to speculate on the future of the new and much more effective TOP Department.

Convention resolutions give at least a surface indication of the problems with which the Union is struggling at any given

[53] *Ibid.,* no. 529, April 27, 1967, p. A-1.
[54] *Ibid.,* no. 676, February 20, 1970, pp. A-4 to A-5, and no. 727, February 12, 1971, pp. C-1 to C-6.

time. In the case of the UAW's white-collar workers these resolutions are now channeled through the TOP advisory council structure.

At the 1966 Long Beach convention these resolutions continued to emphasize automation and bargaining unit erosion. They called for special leadership institutes for white-collar members, and they requested the assignment of a TOP representative to each region to provide improved servicing for white-collar locals. The 1967 Chrysler settlement included a provision for establishing a dispute structure to handle erosion problems and seemed to offer the best prospects to date for this troublesome and continuing problem. Success here can eventually mean an increasing—rather than a nearly stable—white-collar membership in already organized units.

With the wholesale movement of veteran local union leaders into the International Union's administrative structure since 1961, there is now a major gap in the grass-roots leadership— a leadership which played such a central role in the entire revitalization of the UAW's white-collar effort through the ETO caucus and its 1962 program and activity. The development of a new crop of local leaders is perhaps the key to another surge of innovation and expanded interest by the UAW in the white-collar field. Local union leadership training thus assumes central importance at this point.

Interview materials in 1968 indicated that, although important gains were made after 1962 in the quality of servicing available to white-collar local unions and their members, there was still dissatisfaction and room for improvement in this area. The sharp increase in UAW dues in 1967 should permit long-run upgrading in servicing, staff, and bargaining activities by the UAW.

The local leadership gap seems an implicit limitation of white-collar life in the UAW conventions after the 1962 convention "leap." Delegate Bud Lawson, Local 412, seemed concerned by this in his remarks to the 1964 convention:

> Two years ago we came down here with ETO, we came away
> with the TOP Department, and I wish that the ETO group

would get together again to advise the TOP Department in Michigan. But we have the TOP Advisory Council now, and I feel that the ETO group should be advising us on what we want so that we can go back to Brother Fraser and his delegates and get what we need to make this department big.[55]

Thus, in terms of both the objective record and interviews with informed white-collar participants, it seems clear that the TOP advisory council either has not yet been able to find the way to continue the ETO's pioneering functions, or is perhaps inherently incapable of assuming such a role. It seems imperative that an answer to this dilemma must soon be forthcoming if the UAW white-collar effort is to continue as a dynamic, transforming movement. Only two desirable alternatives exist: the advisory councils must become politically active, or a parallel but independent white-collar caucus must once again emerge.

The Need for Education

One of the keys to enhancing the indispensable political support of blue-collar leaders for the Union's white-collar efforts is basically that of education within the Union. The problem demands a thorough and continuing program aimed at increasing the understanding between the two groups within the union. Yet despite the obvious need for such a program in 1961, the UAW Education Department had still failed to structure and implement such a specialized program by 1972. At the 1964 convention, the Education Committee's report went far beyond the scope of the Education Department's own report in elaborating upon "Interesting White-Collar and Technical Workers in Joining the UAW." It pointed out:

A generation ago there existed in the United States and Canada a tragic division between skilled and unskilled workers. This division held back progress of both groups for many years and was ended only by the formation of the CIO and the eventual merger of AFL and CIO.

[55] UAW, *Proceedings, 19th Constitutional Convention, Atlantic City, N.J.,* March 20–27, 1964, p. 464.

Today an equally tragic division of workers is plaguing us: the division between blue-collar and white-collar workers.

We in the UAW have a double incentive for ending this division: one of mutual brotherhood and one of mutual survival.

. . . .

We urge the Education Department to develop new programs that will familiarize blue-collar members of the UAW with the problems of the unorganized white-collar workers.

We further urge the Department to develop programs for white-collar workers who are UAW members to encourage them into full participation in all aspects of our Union's work.[56]

Unfortunately, although the Education Department report to the 1966 convention explicitly acknowledged the 1964 convention's mandate in this regard, the programs which it detailed in subsequent pages revealed no mention of any such program especially directed at the white-collar problem and the needs of the white-collar group.[57] The same deficiency characterized the report of the Education Department to the 1968 and 1970 conventions.[58]

How Much "Will to Organize"?

Although the history of the UAW demonstrates a continued concern for white-collar organizing beginning in the 1930's, the intensity of that interest has been variable, and at times minimal. Thus it is conceivable that the present white-collar effort could again be deemphasized and funds directed elsewhere.

In this connection it is revealing to note that a rough estimate of the "break-even point" for white-collar organizing—the point at which organizing might in some sense be considered to be a

[56] *Ibid.*, p. 225.

[57] See UAW, *Report of President Walter P. Reuther to the 20th Constitutional Convention,* p. 181.

[58] UAW, *Proceedings, 21st Constitutional Convention, Atlantic City, N.J.,* May 4–10, 1968, pp. 425–449. Also see UAW, *Report of President Walter P. Reuther to the 22nd Constitutional Convention, Atlantic City, N.J.,* April 20–25, 1970, Part Two, pp. 133–141.

self-financing operation—would be around 10,000 new members per year, according to union sources. The figure is probably too high, as it neglects continued dues income derived from such members in later years. Generally, it appears to cost approximately twice as much to organize a white-collar worker as it does to organize a blue-collar worker.[59]

Thus it is important to note that the 1967 organizing figures showed a total membership increment of more than 5,000. Hence, on this basis, the TOP Department was approximately half-way to self-sustaining growth in that year.

The possibility that the UAW commitment in this field could be withdrawn was perhaps implicit in the TOP advisory council resolution directed to the 1966 convention. It called for a long-range organizing policy "which will not be deterred by temporary setbacks nor discouraged by failure to gain early elections."[60]

An earlier remark by the department director, Douglas Fraser, is also appropriate here: "We must gear our thinking, and our efforts, to a task which will be a long-range one, an arduous one and a continuing one."[61]

How Deep a Commitment?

In 1963, as a result of earlier analysis of the UAW white-collar problem, I wrote: "In five years, if the UAW has the will to make the necessary adaptations and to commit the substantial resources required, significant gains [appear] to be possible."[62] I also pointed out that "the indispensable ingredient of will, however, has not yet been demonstrated by the UAW in the white-collar area."

The 1962 convention stated the issue in terms that are still

[59] Interview data by author.

[60] *White-Collar Report,* no. 472, March 24, 1966, pp. A-4 to A-5.

[61] See UAW, *Report of President Walter P. Reuther to the 19th Constitutional Convention,* p. 181.

[62] See Carl Dean Snyder, "Industrial Unions Can Lose the Battle for the White-Collar Worker: The UAW as a Case in Point," (D.S.Sc. dissertation, Syracuse University, 1964), pp. 263–264.

intensely relevant: "The question remains—do we have the will, the good sense, and the unity of purpose needed . . . to commit adequate resources equal to the dimensions of the job that must be done?"[63]

Since 1961, the TOP Department and its leadership have succeeded in qualitative as well as quantitative improvements basic to meeting the needs of the existing UAW white-collar membership. It has, at the same time, demonstrated beyond question a markedly improved performance in white-collar organizing. The TOP Department has recruited and developed increasingly skilled personnel, has successfully innovated in the areas of communication, structure, and organizing techniques and strategy, and gives every promise of continued future growth.

Thus the UAW's new white-collar department now represents a means by which developing broad-scale organizing opportunities, within an improved national white-collar context, could be exploited by the Union in a way that it never did in earlier years. The potential scope of white-collar organization within the UAW's jurisdiction is given by the union's estimate of a possible total of 337,000 members.[64]

A Clear Political Problem

The very success of the TOP Department effort to date gives an increasing note of urgency to UAW decisions about white-collar organizing. Both within and outside the UAW there is every evidence that white-collar workers can be and are being organized. This can often be done by industrial unions, so there is no longer any refuge for industrial union leaders in raising the question of possibility in order to defer increasing commitments of staff and funds. Thus the basically political nature of the problem becomes sharply defined.

What is the depth of the International Union leadership's commitment to organizing in general and, in particular, to

[63] See UAW, *Proceedings, 16th Constitutional Convention*, p. 181.
[64] UAW, *Report of President Walter P. Reuther to the 21st Constitutional Convention, Atlantic City, N.J.*, May 4–10, 1968, Part 2, p. 147.

white-collar organizing in those jurisdictions immediately within its control? Second, to what extent is the potential "lead of deliberate change" inherently limited and restrained by "the lag of adversely affected interests" within the UAW?[65] Can political support among blue-collar union leaders at every level in corporations (such as Ford) be mobilized to mount the type of massive and sustained organizing effort required for a strategic breakthrough? Is this possible even at the risk of some cost—at least in the short run—to blue-collar bargaining relationships with the companies involved?[66]

[65] Arthur B. Shostak and William Gomberg, eds., *The Blue-Collar World: Studies of the American Worker* (Englewood Cliffs, N.J.: Prentice-Hall, 1964), p. xv.

[66] This is not peculiar to the UAW. "Delegates to the International Union of Electrical Workers IUE-Professional, Technical, and Salaried Conference Board's annual meeting . . . cited as their most persistent white-collar organizing problem a general lack of support from organized production and maintenance units." See *White-Collar Report,* no. 640, June 12, 1969, p. A-1.

The White-Collar
UAW Member

7

Craft unions such as the Office and Professional Employees International Union have repeatedly charged that industrial unions are unable to meet the special needs of white-collar workers and that they should, therefore, withdraw from organizing competition.

This view has doubtful validity, in an absolute sense. On the other hand, if the particular industrial union is apathetic and unprogressive, the craft unions' charge may be partially true.

The experience of the UAW in the white-collar field clearly refutes the generalization in its more sweeping form. For thirty years the Union has served as the bargaining agent for a sizable group of white-collar employees. Even before 1961 its white-collar membership received servicing and representation adequate enough that there was no important attempt to disaffiliate or decertify white-collar units.

In spite of the frustrations which gave rise to the formation of the ETO caucus, interviews with both local union leaders and rank-and-file white-collar members before 1961 gave no hint of dissatisfaction strong enough to cause white-collar secession. Following the improvements initiated in 1962 and 1963, white-collar members in the UAW actually enjoyed a superior bargaining position because of their affiliation with massive blue-collar strength. This position is one which white-collar employees in the small and struggling "pure white-collar" craft unions will be many years in building.

UAW white-collar units are autonomous. Their leadership is indigenous and originates in the very offices in which members work. In the advisory councils the structure and opportunity now exist to encourage maximum communication and consultation between white-collar units. These councils also facilitate bargaining coordination, provide white-collar representation within the International Union, and stimulate white-collar political life within the Union.

The TOP Department offers specialized white-collar servicing assistance by highly competent staff members with occupational backgrounds in office, technical, and professional employment. A certain amount of specialized white-collar economic and contract analysis can also be secured by local unions. The highly attractive "package" of UAW-negotiated benefits supplies a foundation "pattern" which white-collar members can modify as necessary to meet their particular desires, and the resulting contract is theirs to accept or reject under constitutional guarantees within the Union.

In relation to the issue of craft versus the industrial approach to organizing, consider the position of white-collar UAW members at the local level, including both local union leaders and "actives" and the always more typical "inactives."

Views of Local Union Leaders

The characteristics of white-collar union members are approachable through the eyes of local union leaders. At this level the Union's secondary leadership is in direct daily contact with problems on the job, is in at the origin of grievances, and is immediately accessible to the rank-and-file. The outside observer is always amazed at the dedicated service performed by these indispensable local union people, as Sayles and Strauss have abundantly confirmed.[1]

In interviews the leaders of white-collar UAW local unions in the Detroit area were unanimously convinced of the uniqueness

[1] Leonard R. Sayles and George Strauss, *The Local Union* (New York: Harper and Row, 1953).

of white-collar workers as union members. As a corollary, these local union officers held that a considerable part of the white-collar organizing problem involved the basic attitudes held by these employees. This emphasis suggests that attitude studies might be generally useful in guiding the modification of union structure, adapting union organizing techniques, and, perhaps, in conducting certain critical organizing campaigns.

Regarding these attitudes, local union leaders noted that the white-collar worker desires to have his bargaining representatives look the part, both in meeting with the company and in conducting local union meetings. The white-collar member also wants his representatives to treat the boss with respect. This member typically frowns upon the table-pounding approach to presenting demands, and he is inclined to favor a solution of disputes that will be best for both parties.

Clerical worker unions appeared to accomplish their work somewhat more smoothly, efficiently, and with less emotionality than would have been true of comparable shopworker union meetings. (The avoidance of profanity was likewise a quite noticeable difference.)

Local leaders saw job security as highly valued by white-collar workers, particularly clerical groups. The white-collar employee tends to become deeply convinced of his job's indispensability to the company. Therefore a definite psychological shock is experienced when that job is eliminated by automation or other labor-saving changes in methods.

In nearly every instance local union leaders had an intense personal commitment to increase organizing activity by the International Union. This commitment seemed based upon a dedication to union ideology, but it also derived from economic reality. Bargaining gains at Chrysler were implicitly restrained by the open shop conditions maintained at General Motors and Ford. In an economic pinch this lack of wider organization could jeopardize gains already secured at the Chrysler Corporation.

Recruiting White-Collar Leaders

According to these local leaders, much more reliance must be placed upon service and duty motivations in recruiting white-collar members to serve as officers (and committeemen and stewards) than is typical in the production local union. This is necessary because of the lack of financial and/or working condition differentials that normally operate as incentives to union participation in the shop.

The turnover among white-collar local union officers and committeemen was held to be considerably higher than in the usual blue-collar local union. Local officers noted that this turnover results in a wider diffusion of leadership skills and in a better understanding of union operations by the total membership.

In general, these impressions confirm those of Seidman and Cain in their study of professional engineers and chemists and their observation that full-time union employment was not the same "ladder of success" that it is for blue-collar workers.[2]

Local Union Education

The extensive program of leadership education sponsored by the large amalgamated white-collar office and technical locals is a significant commentary upon the potential of this group. Strong local union interest in education is expressed both through independently planned and executed programs and through those held in cooperation with the International Union and with university extension services.

Membership education is promoted by attractive, interesting, local union newspapers published monthly for all members of the larger white-collar units. These local publications, along with special presentations and daily telephone contact, provide a

[2] Joel Seidman and Glen G. Cain, "Unionized Engineers and Chemists: A Case Study of a Professional Union," *Journal of Business,* July, 1964, p. 245.

continuing upward communication of local officers' view-points to the TOP Department and other servicing agencies of the International Union.

A unique illustration of such local union educational initiative was the 1963 establishment of the Local 412 Technical Training Center. Local union officers successfully designed the project and secured the cooperation of both the International Union and the U.S. Department of Labor. It was "the first significant contract entered into by the government with a labor union to provide training in technical occupations, as well as assisting in up-grading the skills of white-collar employees who stand a chance of being displaced by office automation."[3]

The training center offered classes in mechanical drafting, graphic illustration, and industrial clay modeling. A total of forty hours of evening instruction was offered in each field.

The Durable Difference

The role of white-collar attitudes and group consciousness (which has been noted above in the reactions of unorganized employees and in the testimony of local union leaders) was also verified in discussions with active white-collar union members.

Some quantitative analysis was applied to interview data obtained from a group of twenty-eight active white-collar union members. The term "active" was applied to members who were serving as local union or unit officers, committeemen, and stewards. It was also applied to those who attended membership meetings regularly and/or took part in standing committee activity.

The great preponderance of responses here identified significant, specific differences in the characteristics of white-collar members. In relation to unionism, blue-collar workers were seen as more militant while the white-collar worker was identified more strongly with management. There was strong emphasis upon the rationality and superior education and individualism of the white-collar group, and there was an important component

[3] See *TOP Reporter,* October, 1963, pp. 1, 4.

of class feeling: white-collar workers seemed more concerned about prestige, proper language, and avoiding violence.

The White-Collar Job

White-collar uniqueness was also reflected in the active unionists' identification of the job goals of members. In addition to the common desire for job security and money, there was again the mention of prestige, advancement, recognition from the boss, intellectual stimulation, variety, and personal challenge. An interesting trait of local union actives may be implied from the fact that this group rated white-collar interest in job security much higher than it was actually placed by both inactive and unorganized white-collar workers. Among active unionists 50 percent mentioned this element, as compared to 14 percent of inactive members and 13 percent of unorganized white-collar workers.

The group's identification of white-collar job dislikes gave top position to extremely routine, monotonous work. Next in order were incompetent supervision, the feeling that advancement was impossible, and favoritism.

Participation in the Union

A revealing measure of the response of white-collar workers to unionism is their involvement in union affairs. If those who hold that white-collar workers do not need unionism and find it inherently repugnant were correct, white-collar unions, once established, should have great difficulty maintaining themselves and securing membership support. The evidence regarding office and technical people is entirely to the contrary in the present study.

Taking the level of normal attendance of blue-collar workers at union meetings as 5 percent, it was the opinion of 68 percent of the active unionists interviewed that white-collar attendance was consistently above this level.[4] Another 24 percent felt that

[4] Sayles and Strauss mention attendance figures of 2% to 8% of total membership at membership meetings. This has also been my experience, and that of

such participation was at least as good as that of blue-collar members. Only 8 percent said their fellow members were less inclined to participate than blue-collar people.[5]

Lipset notes, in this connection, that greater democracy in trade union affairs is most frequently found in high-status unions.[6] He likewise suggests that participation tends to be greater among near-middle-class memberships.[7]

Significantly, this evaluation of white-collar participation levels was directly confirmed by interview data drawn from the more typical inactive members.

Attitudes of Inactive Members

One measure of the Union's accomplishment in the white-collar area is the active membership and alert leadership which has developed among this group of unionists. Another measure is to be found in the degree of support gained by the UAW among the more typical, predominant group of inactive union members.

Inactive unionists were considered to be those who did not attend union meetings regularly and were neither stewards, committeemen, nor officers in their local union. Twenty-two were interviewed in this portion of the total sample.

To what extent can, and do, such members adjust to the

---

other observers at blue-collar local union meetings. See Sayles and Strauss, *The Local Union,* p. 121.

[5] Murray Hausknecht notes: "The working class does not join associations in any great numbers." See "The Blue-Collar Joiner," in Arthur B. Shostak and William Gomberg, eds., *The Blue-Collar World: Studies of the American Worker* (Englewood Cliffs, N.J.: Prentice-Hall, 1964), p. 208.

[6] "The obvious conclusions of this analysis are that the functional requirements for democracy cannot be met most of the time in most unions . . . the conflict between democratic and achievement norms means that democracy can exist as a stable system in unions only where the status differentiation between leaders and followers is very small." See Sayles and Strauss, *The Local Union,* p. 121.

[7] He states: "The closer a working-class group approximates a middle-class way of life and orientation the more likely it is to show a high level of union participation." See S. M. Lipset, "The Political Process in Trade Unions," Ch. 4, in Morroe Berger, Theodore Abel, and Charles Page, eds., *Freedom and Control in Modern Society* (New York: Van Nostrand, 1954), p. 104.

union institution where that union is an industrial one composed of an overwhelming majority of blue-collar workers?

As noted elsewhere, unorganized white-collar workers express a strong sense of group difference when they compare themselves to blue-collar employees. An extended period of contact with union ideology and functioning does not eliminate this consciousness of difference.

The inactive group's evaluation of white-collar and blue-collar differences was quite similar to that of the unorganized and the actives. Seventy-three percent of inactive white-collar union members answered affirmatively the question, "Do you see any

TABLE 7–1. INACTIVE MEMBERS'
EVALUATION OF JOB IMPORTANCE

Question: How important is your job to
the success of the company?

Very important	67%
Fairly important	14%
Unimportant	19%

important differences between white-collar workers and shop-workers as groups?" Twenty-seven percent did not recognize such differences. Interestingly, this group was similarly characterized by a strong interest in moving up in the occupational hierarchy.

Something of the inherent self-regard of the white-collar worker is also conveyed by his view of the importance of his own job. The data in Table 7–1 are relevant here.

Presumably the incidence of white-collar organization would tend to be greater where routine jobs predominated. Thus it appears especially noteworthy that, even here, more than 80 percent of this group of unionized white-collar workers evaluated their jobs as at least fairly important to the success of the company.

In answer to the question, "In general, do you feel that whatever is in the best interests of your employer is also usually best for you?" interviewees indicated agreement in 71 percent of the cases. Thus certain white-collar attitudes and characteristics which differ significantly from those of blue-collar employees continue nearly unchanged despite years of union membership.

"Inactives" Look at the Union

Evidence of the UAW's success in meeting white-collar needs can be discerned in interviews with inactive members. As a group, these members were less concerned about union power and union militance than were unorganized white-collar interviewees, and they were much more inclined to accept the UAW as their representative than to prefer a solely white-collar union. There was also a sharp decrease in the percentage of those who felt that union membership necessarily implies a loss of prestige.

The UAW received better-than-average ratings from its own members when it was compared with other unions. Table 7–2 shows the relevant data.

TABLE 7–2. INACTIVE MEMBERS'
OPINIONS OF THE UAW

Question: What is your opinion of the
UAW as compared to other unions?

Better than other unions	65%
About the same as other unions	30%
Not as good as other unions	0%
No clear opinion held	5%

This rating of the UAW is substantially higher than that given the Union by unorganized white-collar workers in the industry. In comparison, the unorganized employees included only 39 percent who felt that the UAW was better than other unions. This fact certainly supports the view that the UAW has been basically successful in its efforts to serve and to integrate white-collar workers. White-collar experience in the UAW produced attitudes and associations related to unions which were substantially more favorable to the Union than were those of unorganized white-collar employees.[8]

An alternative explanation is that of selection. However, since the interviewees were in long-established units which had been

[8] Also see Ch. 2.

exposed to extensive mixing through transfer and to long, continued turnover and attrition, the selection hypothesis offers a much more strained explanation.

Acceptable Leadership

Just as in the case of the unorganized white-collar group, inactive members expressed high regard for the top leadership of the Union. Interviewees responding to a question requesting a specific opinion of UAW President Walter Reuther gave him strong commendation. Eighty-three percent praised the UAW leader for "intelligent, effective representation of workers"; 39 percent specifically mentioned his honesty and conscientiousness; 22 percent were impressed by his articulateness. In contrast, only 6 percent disapproved of this articulateness and 6 percent doubted his capability as a leader.

Interview results here indicated that white-collar workers, once introduced to unionism and participating on a limited basis in its activities, are converted to a much more favorable view of the union and its services than that held by unorganized white-collar workers who have a largely secondhand knowledge of unionism. This tendency was sharply illustrated in a summary question: "Considering present-day conditions, do you think that unions are necessary for salaried and other white-collar workers?" Sixty-seven percent indicated agreement. This contrasted with 14 percent of unorganized white-collar interviewees who felt unions were necessary for white-collar workers. Again, the selection hypothesis does not seem an adequate explanation. Interviews demonstrated that the UAW has achieved and maintained commanding support for unionization among this group of white-collar workers.

The Participation Potential of White-Collar Members

Although by definition this group of members was not actively participating in union affairs, interviewees nevertheless showed a strong willingness to support the Union in a number of ways beyond their present role. Table 7–3 shows the data.

Note the sharp reversal between the inactive members' acceptance of committee participation and their rejection of the responsibilities of serving as an officer of the union. The willingness to accept picket-line duty is likewise noteworthy—and, not unexpectedly, substantially above that of unorganized white-collar workers. Again, this serves to support the hypothesis concerning assimilation in the Union.

However, this characteristic willingness to participate in organizational affairs was also a prominent aspect of the attitudes of unorganized white-collar workers. In that group, 45 percent indicated a willingness, once unionized, to serve on a union committee; 65 percent were willing to serve on a picket line.

TABLE 7–3. INACTIVE MEMBERS' ATTITUDES TOWARD UNION PARTICIPATION

Question: I am interested in the extent of your willingness to co-operate with the union. For example, consider the following possibilities. Would you be willing to:

	Yes	No
Serve on a union committee if chosen by your fellow workers	69%	32%
Hold office in the union, if you were elected by your fellow workers	36%	64%
In case of a strike, to serve on a picket line	95%	5%

Moving from speculative possibilities to reality, data were sought concerning the actual participation of interviewees in the events of the November, 1958, white-collar strike at the Chrysler Corporation. Seventy-seven percent indicated that they had personally participated in the strike activity.

Various reasons were offered for individual participation. These included "a requirement by the Union" (because of strike benefits), novelty, duty, and a desire to help. There was no instance of a respondent indicating that he had absolutely refused to cooperate, although several had been excused for illness. Two respondents indicated that they had felt compelled to participate and expressed some resentment at the necessity involved.

White-Collar Strike Action

Frequently in the past it was assumed that white-collar workers would not strike. For example, William Lange asks, "Can you imagine white-collar people being willing to picket"[9] Both the experience of existing UAW white-collar units and the present interview study contradict the answer implied by that previous question. The rash of teachers' strikes in recent years is additional confirmation.

In sum, it appears certain that a union can expect entirely adequate support from its white-collar members in those crisis situations where a strike becomes necessary. In less dramatic circumstances, white-collar unionism offers the possibility of a relatively high degree of membership interest and participation.

White-Collar Bargaining Differences

For the most part, the central economic interests of white-collar members are very similar to the blue-collar unionists' goals. Thus, as exemplified by the discussion of Chrysler bargaining in the preceding chapter, there is a common core of bargaining demands which both groups will support. "Once organized, white-collar groups seem to negotiate agreements that show more similarities than differences when compared to manual workers' agreements."[10]

One of the central institutions of unionism, the grievance procedure, seems little understood or desired by unorganized white-collar workers. Once workers are organized, however, this procedure becomes familiar and valued even among the higher reaches of white-collar professionals.[11]

[9] See William H. Lange, "Target for Tomorrow: The White-Collar Employee," *Office Executive,* February, 1958, pp. 14–18.

[10] Everett M. Kassalow, "White-Collar Unionism in the United States," in Adolf Sturmthal, ed., *White-Collar Trade Unions* (Urbana: University of Illinois Press, 1966), p. 362.

[11] See James W. Kuhn, "Success and Failure in Organizing Professional Engineers," *Proceedings of Sixteenth Annual Meeting* (Madison, Wis.: Industrial Relations Research Association, 1964), p. 208.

This said, it is important to note the points at which these interests do diverge. It is difficult to evaluate the importance of this divergence, although it appears that both craft unions and management typically exaggerate it.

One area where the difference is clear is in the somewhat greater acceptance of merit criteria which characterizes white-collar attitudes. Kassalow suggests that "even after unionization,

TABLE 7–4. INACTIVE MEMBERS AND THE SENIORITY ISSUE IN PROMOTION

Question: How important should merit be—as compared to seniority or length of service—when promoting a white-collar person?

	Total	Technical	Clerical
Merit should be primary; emphasizes individual initiative	32%	58%	0%
Merit first, but would consider seniority	32%	33%	30%
Each factor should have equal weight	9%	8%	10%
Seniority first, but should consider merit	18%	0%	40%
Seniority primary; emphasizes favoritism; need for job security	5%	0%	10%
Other	5%	0%	10%

they continue to feel that merit should count heavily in promotion. It is part of their professional identification. . . . What professional workers seek and what organization can and must offer is a system in which merit can operate with fair objectivity."[12]

My study provided definite evidence that this factor was directly correlated with the progression from routine clerical functions to the highly skilled technical and engineering occupations. Interview results concerning the seniority versus merit issue in promotion are shown in Table 7–4.

[12] Harold J. Gibbons, Everett M. Kassalow, and Joel Seidman, "Developments in White Collar Unionism," *Occasional Papers, No. 24* (Chicago: University of Chicago Industrial Relations Center, 1962), p. 9.

Inactive members seem to have almost the same interest in the merit criterion as do unorganized workers. There is little indication here that union experience has modified the typical white-collar member's attitudes on this particular issue.

However, when inactive members in technical occupations are contrasted with those in clerical occupations, there is a striking difference in their commitment to the merit principle. This is apparent in the second and third columns of Table 7–4. On probing, this seemed to reflect an awareness of the central role of individual talent in certain types of creative work in the design field.

Despite the persisting support for the inclusion of merit in promotion decisions at higher levels, white-collar workers interviewed seemed nearly unanimous in favoring seniority as the determining element in establishing the order of layoff. The unorganized worker portion of the total sample was inclined to allow the company an exceptionally long "probationary" period before the seniority standard would govern, even here. Seidman and Cain, however, report a rejection of the seniority criterion as the layoff standard among a group of professional engineers and chemists.[13]

The Union Shop

American unions are strongly characterized by their concern for organizational security through making membership a contractual requirement. As one moves along a continuum from production worker to professional, there may be an increasing reluctance to accept compulsory membership. Among the professional engineers and chemists cited just above, "Opposition to anything but an open shop was almost unanimous."[14] As noted below, this was the conviction of Minneapolis-Honeywell professionals also.

Among the unorganized interviewees in my study 57 percent indicated that they did not favor a union-shop contract arrange-

[13] Seidman and Cain, "Unionized Engineers and Chemists," p. 246.
[14] *Ibid.*

ment. Thirty-five percent favored this form of union security, while 9 percent took an intermediate position. Responses in the inactive UAW member group expressed much more support for the union shop arrangement. Here 71 percent favored compulsory membership and 29 percent were opposed.

This apparent shift in viewpoint seems best explained as an indication of the marginal nature of this issue. A newly organized local first gives priority to other bargaining goals. The desirability of comprehensive coverage of the unit ultimately becomes apparent. Membership support then permits local union leaders and International representatives to push for a union security clause. The limiting situation here is probably that of the professional employee group.

Political Action

There is evidence from studies of comparative unionism, as seen in Europe and elsewhere, that white-collar unions tend toward political conservatism.[15] This was likewise the conclusion of a valuable report prepared by a UAW leadership team that visited Europe in 1959.[16]

Political activities of the Union constitute a negative, but not crucial, factor in relation to the unionization of unorganized white-collar workers. This same fact appeared in interviews with inactive white-collar union members.

There was some ambivalence in this area. Here the Union's legislative programs were differentiated favorably from its efforts to secure the election of particular candidates. Thus 64 percent of respondents stated that they did not carefully consider the Union's political recommendations regarding candidates for public office. Their explanations on this point showed nearly half of the group making an explicit statement that they were

[15] See Adolf Sturmthal, "White-Collar Unions—A Comparative Essay," in Sturmthal, ed., *White-Collar Trade Unions,* p. 385.

[16] Victor Reuther, Robert Shebal, and Irving Bluestone, "Report on Special Mission to Selected European Countries to Study White-Collar Worker Organization, March 16 to April 10, 1959" (Detroit: International UAW-AFL-CIO, July, 1959).

politically independent. Thirty-one percent indicated a strong rejection of the Union's political recommendations here as interference. This was supported at another point by opinions of 27 percent of the sample group who denied that unions had a right to take part in the election of candidates to public office. An additional fifth of the sample indicated mixed feelings.

One-fourth to one-third of inactive UAW white-collar members interviewed were critical of the Union's political activities to some degree. However, for most members this criticism did not involve intense emotional disapproval. The explanation seemed to be that most members (65%) approved the overall legislative program of the Union.

Thus the political action issue among white-collar workers is much less critical than has been generally assumed. In the present study there was no clear polarization around either strongly opposing or strongly supporting extremes. There does not appear to be any intense and strongly principled rejection of union activity in the political arena.

Individual interviews with local union leaders and TOP Department personnel verified the existence of a membership split on political issues and candidates. In general, local union policy seemed either to follow a somewhat cautious bipartisan approach or else to minimize exhortation and political activity. To the extent that the latter is felt to be necessary to unity, it suggests that, as the UAW's white-collar membership becomes proportionately more important, a substantially increased program of educational persuasion will be required.

Would-be Capitalists?

In summarizing the bargaining goals of the TOP Department, the white-collar interest in an improved stock thrift plan emerged. At various points before the 1967 negotiations in the auto industry, the UAW leadership tentatively explored profit-sharing. From interviews with white-collar actives and other members, as well as with International Union staff members, it seems that stock acquisition is very much a live issue with white-collar members. At present, blue-collar support for this type of benefit is lagging, but ultimately there is the possibility that present stock plans in some white-collar agreements will attract general union interest and support.

A Possible Agenda
for Industrial Unions:
The Significance of the
UAW Experience

8

The 1971 *Manpower Report of the President* states that the manpower requirements of the United States in 1975 will demand 51 percent white-collar workers but only 33 percent blue-collar employees. The projections indicate that service workers will constitute about 16 percent of the labor force.[1]

Either this continuing white-collar drift will force the organizing efforts of blue-collar industrial unions to become, as the UAW's Irving Bluestone so succinctly phrases it, a "two-front" effort to include both groups of employees, or industrial unions must become relatively less influential within the labor movement and the society. Reece McGee's comment is appropriate here: "It is entirely possible that the industrial unions . . . will decline, and unionism will become a reactionary defender of past privileges rather than a harbinger of the future."[2]

Based on an extensive analysis of UAW experience, I conclude that, although white-collar organizing is quite difficult and complex, industrial unions can successfully operate in this area. To do so requires explicit, conscious adaptation on the part of the union, as developments in the UAW so well demonstrate.

Certainly one of the most meaningful lessons of the UAW's experience is that the required changes are within practical

[1] See U.S. Department of Labor, *Manpower Report of the President* (Washington, D.C., 1971), p. 297.
[2] Reece McGee, "White-Collar Explosion," *Nation*, February 7, 1959, pp. 112–115.

limits in terms of both financial resources and modifications of institutional structure.

Multi-Group Unions?

An important prerequisite to white-collar organizing success is modification of the "mind set" of the traditional blue-collar industrial unionist. S. M. Miller speculates that "the reluctance of labor leaders to organize white-collar workers is pronounced, and may be due to their fear of this kind of well-educated union member as well as to jurisdictional problems."[3] The industrial union seriously interested in white-collar organizing must be willing to accept an administratively inconvenient diversity of structure and flexibility of policy and practice.

Thus the UAW and some other industrial unions have pragmatically moved toward a mixed, multi-group type of structure. In the UAW a major contributing force has been the incipient skilled-trades schism. But significant inter-industry differences such as those between the auto, aerospace, and agricultural implement areas have also developed institutional counterparts within the Union.

For many union leaders the orthodox industrial union ideology can constitute a mental block to effective understanding of the white-collar problem. In its traditional form this ideology seems to inhibit new approaches to the basic dilemma. This reflects itself in a willingness to rely upon such comfortable answers as an irresistible trend toward mechanization and automation, or sheer increase in the numbers of white-collar workers that will inevitably lead to their unionization, or a conversion of white-collar workers which will bring them to recognize the facts of life. In short, there is a dallying hope for an effortless solution to the industrial union's problem through changes in *external* circumstances. These changes would make the standard methods of industrial union organizing relevant again. Fre-

[3] See S. M. Miller, "Some Thoughts on Reform," in Arthur B. Shostak and William Gomberg, eds., *The Blue-Collar World: Studies of the American Worker* (Englewood Cliffs, N.J.: Prentice-Hall, 1964) p. 305.

quently this view has led to impassioned appeals for re-creating the missionizing spirit of the 1930's—despite the disappearance of the intensely supportive circumstances of that historical period.

In this regard, the ideology of industrial unionism may be as potentially limiting in its influence upon the unions' ability to adapt to the changing circumstances of its present environment as was true earlier of craft unionism. One recalls that industrial unionists roundly condemned a similar failing of craft union leaders as short-sighted and impractical in the middle 1930's.

As Sturmthal points out, "Fundamental changes in the structure of the labor force have always led to basic readjustment of the structure and the policies of the labor movement."[4] Veteran labor leaders may yearn for a rebirth of the missionizing spirit of old and, nostalgically, for the simple blacks and whites of their stubborn resistance to management brutality in the 1930's. Yet this hardly constitutes the basis for a successful organizing program geared to modern problems in an ever more complicated economy. Thus it seems to follow that the labor leader who has not grown and adapted his thinking and methods in pace with the sophisticated technology that management now applies both to the product and to personnel problems is obsolete.

Organizing across Class Lines

The white-collar organizing problem facing the industrial union is that of finding effective means of organizing across a class "barrier," albeit a permeable one in the United States.

The basic framework of analysis which I have been developing underlies the discussion in this chapter. My primary assumption is that white-collar "difference" is real and persisting. The white-collar worker has a certain self-image which he values highly. Some aspects of his view of unions are in conflict with this self-image. The most malleable element is the image of the

---

[4] Adolf Sturmthal, "White-Collar Unions—A Comparative Essay," in Adolf Sturmthal, ed., *White-Collar Trade Unions* (Urbana: University of Illinois Press, 1966), p. 397.

union; this image is subject both to recasting by changes in the union and its actions and to more accurate projection by the union and its organizing staff. The union will be accepted as a means to white-collar ends if the images are perceived as sufficiently compatible in the mind of the white-collar worker. The minimum necessary congruence of these images will be modified by the sum of favoring and inhibiting influences in the specific organizing situation, and less immediately—but in the long run importantly—by the larger context of events in the economy and the social order.[5]

The Limits of Required Change

Now to consider the specific changes that white-collar organizing may require of the industrial union. I shall examine the limits of those changes, the highlights of UAW experience in this area, and, in the next chapter, some additional areas for industrial union experimentation.

The modifications required of industrial unions in the white-collar field are finite and within the realm of practicality. Kassalow's comment that there must be "a major transformation of much of the institution itself" is useful in its emphasis but too sweeping in its demand.[6]

The initial need for funds is modest. Attempts to meet the white-collar problem by a massive outpouring of union resources—channeled through an inadequate organizing department using inappropriate organizing techniques—are predestined to failure. But once union readiness is attained by some internal reorganization, increased funds should be allocated. Then the union's efforts can be steadily stepped up in appro-

---

[5] Lombardi and Grimes suggest a model using four causal variables: the social and economic situation as perceived by the white-collar worker, leadership, public policy, and the threshold level of unionization for the group. Their model highlights a different portion of the relevant elements than does our own. It seems, however, to be less adaptable to use in analyzing organizing problems. See Vincent Lombardi and Andrew Grimes, "A Primer for a Theory of White-Collar Unionization," *Monthly Labor Review*, May, 1967, pp. 46–49.

[6] Everett M. Kassalow, "New Union Frontier: White-Collar Workers," *Harvard Business Review*, January–February, 1962, p. 51.

priate relation to the white-collar potential within its jurisdiction.

The perspective required is that of a long-term investment in the future of modern industrial unionism and in the future of the specific union involved. Necessary changes may consume three to seven years before sharply improved organizing performance appears. Short-term reverses and mistakes should be expected and discounted. Substantial subsidization from the union's general funds must be accepted as indispensable. At least during the initial period of organizing, it may cost roughly twice as much to organize a white-collar worker as a blue-collar worker.

The Lessons of the UAW Experience

Before considering some additional possibilities for improved industrial union performance in the white-collar field, it is instructive to analyze further the UAW experience detailed particularly in Chapter Six: how one industrial union moved from inertia and ineffectiveness in the white-collar area to an alert and increasingly successful office and technical organizing operation.

The industrial unions have differing traditions and leadership; thus the UAW experience can be applied only in large outline and as one demonstration of adaptation. Individual unions must select those features which are appropriate to their own situation.

In the UAW one of the primary conditions which facilitated adaptation was the high degree of internal union democracy.[7] It was within this context that the Engineering-Technical-Office caucus could organize itself, and it was UAW leadership's alertness to membership pressures and desires that brought high-level attention to ETO's requests.

The leadership of the Union was also sufficiently diverse that high-ranking direction of the new white-collar effort was available through an Executive Board member capable of working closely with white-collar local union leadership. The new director

[7] See Jack Stieber, *Governing the UAW* (New York: John Wiley and Sons, 1962), pp. 158–170. He concludes: "On balance the UAW—despite the absence of continual and institutionalized opposition—must be considered a democratic union."

fortunately combined blue-collar background and bargaining expertise with a personality that was effective with white-collar workers.

A 1957 constitutional change offered an organizing asset by allowing white-collar autonomy within the Union in the key matter of contract ratification. Further recommendations for more white-collar choice and decision-making were acceptable to the prime policy-making body of the Union. This expanding autonomy has facilitated both effective servicing and internal administration of white-collar affairs and provided a most significant talking point in organizing campaigns.

The Argument for White-Collar Autonomy

Autonomy for white-collar members of industrial unions is so central to success in this area that a digression is in order to clarify this portion of UAW experience. In 1960 Chrysler white-collar Local 889 pointed out to the International Union's Executive Board that

> the worst deterrent to organizing, and the point most successfully used by management groups is the placement of white-collar workers into production and maintenance units. . . . the most vital and active office and technical groups are those who have remained the masters of their own destiny . . . [if they] are put in a position of being just a small segment of a large mass of workers in the production plants, they are often disgruntled, indifferent, or actively hostile to our union.[8]

Consequently, Local 889 recommended that amalgamated local unions composed of white-collar workers should be established on an area basis. Where thinness of organization makes this impractical, the white-collar group should be made a distinct unit in an amalgamated local union of blue-collar workers.

Autonomous structure fosters a vital white-collar group consciousness within the union. In the UAW existing white-collar

---

[8] Wallace Webber et al., "Analysis of the White-Collar Organizational Problem: Presentation before the UAW International Executive Board" (Detroit: UAW Local 889, January 20, 1960), p. 28.

local unions have identified strongly with the need for further organization. The white-collar locals have demonstrated a striking willingness to make important commitments of money, time, and effort to such organization.[9]

Through autonomy the increased visibility of the white-collar group within the union can well mean an increasing interest on the part of blue-collar members in the white-collar problem. Naturally, this assumes judicious white-collar leadership and participation in convention and other international union activities.

From an administrative standpoint, such a clarified structure makes it much simpler to identify the size and distribution of white-collar membership within the union. The basic trends affecting that membership are easier to analyze. This structure also facilitates specialized communication among white-collar units. Servicing responsibilities can be more clearly delineated and a better quality of specialized service provided.

For this approach to succeed, the common interest of shop and office workers vis-à-vis the employer must be steadily recognized. There must be full cooperation in bargaining at both local and national levels. Responsible leaders of both blue-collar and white-collar groups need to emphasize continuing communication and consultation. Here the basic philosophy of industrial unionism offers a valuable guide to solidarity.

In 1967 the need for white-collar visibility at the level of the national federation was partially met by the formation of the AFL-CIO's Council of Unions for Scientific, Professional, and Cultural Employees (SPACE). But a broader-based organization encompassing all white-collar members would seem to have been a logically prior development—with specialization coming at a later time.[10]

The 1971 International TOP Advisory Council Conference at Black Lake demonstrated the importance of autonomous structure and visibility, as well as the broad scope of white-collar

---

[9] For an example of such cooperation between Local 889 and the International Union, see *White-Collar Report*, no. 160, March 28, 1960, p. A-1.

[10] *Ibid.*, no. 523, March 16, 1967, pp. A-12 to A-14.

union member interests. In addition to bargaining concerns, a considerable portion of the program was essentially of an educational nature—covering legal and civil rights of special groups such as black and women workers, educational needs of white-collar local unions and members, problems of drug and alcohol abuse, youth trends and the universities, insurance programs, consumer problems, and car safety legislation and styling changes.[11]

Two-way Communication

The UAW's leadership has been astute enough to accept and use many of the recommendations and advice formulated by white-collar office and technical local unions. It drew heavily upon local union leaders for an expansion of the white-collar staff of the International Union. It also embarked upon a program of close cooperation with local units for, as Local 889 suggested, the creation of an "organizing reserve" made up of part-time and volunteer organizers.

Obtaining qualified, talented white-collar staff members is of such crucial importance to effective industrial union performance in this area that some further consideration of the problem is desirable.

Personnel

It may be necessary to introduce changes into the industrial unions' personnel policies to attract qualified white-collar workers as staff members. Dedication to white-collar unionization is a legitimate requirement for such individuals, but it is also important to recognize that substantial salary differentials may be needed to overcome the pull of more favorable working conditions in existing white-collar positions in the plant and office. "Leaving the office" offers less motivation than "getting out of

---

[11] See *Minutes of the 4th International T.O.P. Advisory Council Conference held at the Walter and May Reuther Family Education Center, Black Lake, Mich.,* May 26–28, 1971, pp. 3–4.

the shop." This is a problem particularly in the recruitment of engineering and design personnel, who will suffer severely from skill deterioration if they should later attempt to return to their former occupation.[12]

The industrial union is under special pressure to show prospective members that it has the personnel, resources, and know-how to serve adequately the needs of white-collar employees. Thus, for staff members assigned to this area, white-collar background is nearly indispensable, since it colors language, style of dress, and manner—intangibles which are almost impossible to convey in a training program.

Minimum educational qualifications include high school graduation and, probably, additional night school or college preparation. Indeed, one may speculate that white-collar workers might be favorably approached by organizers with an education and language facility superior to their own. This is in sharp contrast to the usual organizing emphasis with blue-collar workers where the attempt is to convey equality: "He's just like us—'one of the boys.' "[13]

Status for Organizers

A major requirement for progress in this area is to find the institutional means to confer increased status upon the white-collar organizing staff. This status must be commensurate with the central importance of the organizing function to the future of the union. Solomon Barkin's observation that formal staff training will be required is clearly correct. The implementation of a career pattern in organizing may well be explored.[14]

[12] Bernard P. Indik and Bernard Goldstein also note the lack of a financial incentive. See their "Professional Engineers Look at Unions," *Proceedings of Sixteenth Annual Meeting* (Madison, Wis.: Industrial Relations Research Association, 1964), p. 215.

[13] I have encountered adverse white-collar reactions to union personnel even because of physically dominating body characteristics. White-collar perception is highly conditioned by media-conveyed stereotypes of unions as users of violence and intimidation.

[14] Solomon Barkin, *Decline of the Labor Movement* (Santa Barbara, Calif.: Center for the Study of Democratic Institutions, 1961), p. 57.

Organizers' morale needs maximum support. Caskey pin-points an important union weakness here; he argues that there is an "underlying belief among many white-collar organizers . . . that the 'white-collar crusade' is doomed to failure."[15]

The more specialized the group of employees with whom the staff member is expected to work, the greater the importance of his having had closely related occupational experience. Professionals are particularly sensitive to and critical of organizers who cannot accurately use the appropriate occupational jargon.

A reserve of volunteer consultants that can be drawn on to work jointly with the full-time staff whenever specialized groups are approached would be a useful resource.

A Structural Requirement

White-collar organizing requires a specialized division in the industrial union (such as the UAW's TOP Department), which can offer leadership as well as specialized servicing and organizing skills and contract research facilities to local units. Perhaps even more important for long-run adaptation is the forming of a specifically white-collar structure for local union collaboration, the maximizing of communication, and the development of group coherence among the white-collar minority.

In the UAW prior to 1961 individual units (with the possible exception of the two large amalgamated locals in Detroit) tended to be isolated and lacked adequate contact with other white-collar local unions, as well as with the International Union. An advisory council structure similar to that established by TOP Department leadership can become one of the key mechanisms for integrating the white-collar group into the affairs of the total union.

Such councils, together with staff contacts, constitute the most effective insurance that unique white-collar views will be formulated and communicated upward to higher-level policy-

[15] Clark Caskey, "White-Collar Employees—A Union Dilemma and a Management Challenge" (Ann Arbor: University of Michigan Bureau of Industrial Relations, March, 1962), p. 4.

makers. In the UAW, the *TOP Reporter,* a primarily white-collar publication, also provides an additional valuable channel for quick communication of white-collar news and information to all units. Such a publication is more effective in disseminating information than in initiating policy. However, it can perform a significantly stimulating role in relation to such policy formation. Creation of policy by specially called white-collar conferences can also be useful, as demonstrated by both the UAW and the Steelworkers.[16]

Possible Organizing Approaches

Finally, UAW white-collar experience is valuable to other industrial unions in providing a still evolving pattern of organizing. It has identified certain types of organizing situations which are particularly likely to offer membership gains.

In organizing techniques, the UAW emphasizes a quick election campaign after achieving the minimum 30 percent authorization card requirement. If defeated, it deliberately returns again and again and is frequently successful on the second or third trial at the same location. It has found Canadian representation procedures favorable to the enlistment of new white-collar members. The Union has frequently made large gains by an alert response to appeals from independently organized associations who find themselves in some type of crisis. Although it sometimes uses house calls, the UAW has found that the most indispensable and effective organizing tool is an active in-plant committee of white-collar employees.

Favorable organizing circumstances identified in UAW experience include a number of specific situations. Pending corporate merger is especially conducive to unionization. The large-scale corporate structure itself has proved an asset for the UAW, for it has often been feasible to expand an initial organizing breakthrough in a particular company unit to include a chain

[16] See especially "Resolutions for Submission to the International Wage Policy Committee of the United Steelworkers of America," 1st International White-Collar Conference, May 11–12, 1967, Chicago, Ill.

of plants and locations. The Union has also found increased white-collar interest in unionization where competitive cost pressures tempt management to "cut corners" with its white-collar overhead, as in supplier firms.

Thus, for other industrial unions, the total UAW experience can be highly instructive and can save a great deal of valuable time in starting effective white-collar organizing.

A Possible Agenda for Industrial Unions: Some Additional Considerations

9

The preceding analysis summarizes UAW reforms in the white-collar field. However, some additional observations can be offered in relation to potential white-collar organizing efforts of industrial unions.

In contrast to the traditionalists, S. M. Miller has argued that unions, if they are to be successful in their entry to the white-collar area "without," must first look "within."[1] This process is demanding. In the last analysis, it appears that the key to a more successful industrial union response to the white-collar challenge lies initially in the minds and attitudes of its leadership and ultimately in those of the blue-collar membership. Only as there is a basic reorientation at these levels can those other changes which are described here be achieved. The white-collar problem is, first of all, a problem in understanding for present industrial union leaders.[2]

The blue-collar unionist must come to accept the legitimacy of white-collar difference. He must make a positive and continuing effort to understand the white-collar viewpoint and value system if he is to overcome white-collar reservations concerning unionism.

[1] This valuable discussion is contained in S. M. Miller's discussion of Everett Kassalow's paper, "Occupational Frontiers of Trade Unionism," *Proceedings of Thirteenth Annual Meeting* (Madison, Wis.: Industrial Relations Research Association, 1961), p. 215.
[2] See, for example, Arthur A. Sloane's remarks as cited in *White-Collar Report*, no. 669, January 1, 1970, pp. A-1 to A-4.

Thus a deliberate program within the union to maximize contacts between blue-collar and white-collar leadership at every level is indicated. Interaction and discussion would be initiated and maintained. Part of this can be consciously emphasized in educational activities within the union. However, placement of staff members with white-collar background and functions within the "old line" union departments will also be useful here.

The White-Collar Value System

The costly derision which blue-collar workers often feel for white-collar values needs to be minimized. Some sources of this are superficial; for example, there is the stereotyped generalization, "White-collar workers are snobs." Personal interaction between white- and blue-collar leaders can attack this misconception, because such snobbery on the part of white-collar union leaders is rare. Manifestations of this attitude were also relatively infrequent among inactive members and unorganized white-collar workers.

Office and technical employees do have a conscious sense of difference. They demonstrate a natural human preference for, and belief in, the superiority of their own way of living, doing things, and making choices. Blue-collar workers have this same type of preference in reverse, finding white-collar values strangely ordered in some respects. However, problems in this connection are usually exaggerated; in reality, they are manageable within a common organization.

On the other hand, in important areas of blue-collar workers' lives there are strong similarities to white-collar values. These often furnish the fundamental basis upon which unionism claims justification—for instance, the appreciation for human dignity and the desire for freedom from arbitrary authority.

White-collar and blue-collar workers' goals are different in important respects. Yet frequently these goals are different primarily because blue-collar workers are still aspiring to certain working conditions which white-collar workers, by historical accident, acquired quite early. White-collar workers who have achieved these objectives are understandably not interested in jeopardizing them or rejecting such gains to attain unity with an apparently less-advantaged group. However, this is not to say that the white-collar worker lives in a utopia where there are no needs or wants which might usefully be served by organization.

The industrial union needs to regard white-collar workers as at a different stage of attainment and aspiration—especially in terms of working conditions—than its blue-collar membership. On the other hand, blue-collar negotiated economic gains have, at certain points, forged ahead of lagging white-collar benefits.

J. P. Fitzpatrick has commented that "the highest values of American life were associated with white-collar work—the association in men's minds of freedom and self-fulfillment is still very strong."[3] Perhaps the most convincing testimony here is blue-collar parents' strong urging that their children get out of the shop and get an education. For what purpose? To qualify for a white-collar job of one type or another, and to move *upward* into the middle class.[4]

Institutional Flexibility

The second point of a possible program of white-collar adaptation by the industrial union would be the evolution of an explicit, conscious set of principles—a philosophy—of institutional flexibility. Miller put the need in these terms: "Kassalow . . . notes that unionism will "probably strengthen and consolidate" the trend toward bureaucratization and standardization of white-collar work. He accepts this as given. Is it? Can unionism prevent arbitrary employer action only by building inflexible regulations?[5]

A number of industrial unions have emphasized internal union

[3] J. P. Fitzpatrick, "The Dilemma of the White-Collar Worker," *Thought*, Summer, 1951, p. 239.

[4] "All of the studies are consistent in showing that the majority of blue-collar workers do not want their children to follow their line of work." See William G. Dyer, "Family Reactions to the Father's Job," in Arthur B. Shostak and William Gomberg, eds., *The Blue-Collar World: Studies of the American Worker* (Englewood Cliffs, N.J.: Prentice-Hall, 1964), p. 90.

[5] See S. M. Miller, "Discussion," p. 215.

democracy. In this tradition it would be useful to experiment with various methods of involving a new type of membership in union programs and decision-making. White-collar members seem to have a characteristically greater rate of participation in union affairs. The white-collar group sets a high store upon the value of education and favors an objective presentation of issues. Thus national education conferences—such as sponsored by the UAW in earlier years—could have great relevance to white-collar unionism. A judicious choice of location for such conferences would also maximize their impact as organizing influences.

From such a philosophy of flexibility and its policy manifestations (which will be examined below) an industrial union can project a highly influential image among white-collar workers. The stereotype of union rigidity and uniformity has a certain residue of actuality. White-collar workers express many apprehensions about these aspects of union functioning.

A Policy Framework

Still at the level of intangible considerations, a third point involves the leadership needs to frame overall union policies with a continuing awareness of their implications for white-collar organizing.

Obviously this cannot and does not mean that the union should forego every decision or act tending to adversely affect white-collar opinion. The industrial union's commitment to its present membership is primary, but this point does imply that the union's blue-collar objectives might often be pursued—and interpreted publicly—in such a way as to minimize the negative reactions of white-collar workers to those acts.

Miller suggests that "it is not management which alone breeds discontent and distrust." To some extent today industrial relations can be viewed as "competition between management and unions as to which can generate *less* discontent and distrust rather than more good will." The difficulty is partly that of the union image. It requires changing the behavior of unions so that the 'propaganda of the deed' carries the message.[6] These internal changes in thought and deed must be followed by a systematic attempt to project a changed concept of the union to the white-collar public.

Policy Areas for Reconsideration

Several traditional policies of industrial unions need to be re-examined in light of their significance for white-collar organizing. The sticking point in many instances is that bureaucratic imperative, uniformity.

First, there is the use of the strike weapon. It seems clear that, contrary to earlier management assumptions, white-collar employees will strike forcefully and effectively where the need is clear and understood. Nevertheless, this instrument tends to be wielded somewhat more reluctantly by white-collar unionists than by shop workers. More adequate and detailed explanation and preparation for such action appears desirable. With some white-collar employees, such as professionals, the use of the strike might be considered only in the most critical situations.

Leadership remarks which could be misinterpreted as evidence of union irresponsibility in this regard have a negative impact on potential members. Reliance upon outside mediation and arbitration procedures can be useful.

The Knotty Problem of Seniority

The industrial union moving into white-collar organizing must devise patterns which guarantee fairness in promotion and insure job security without relying solely upon the traditional seniority system applied in the shop.

From interview materials it seems clear that, in relatively routine clerical jobs, a high degree of white-collar acceptance for the seniority standard exists, or can be attained by the union over a period of time.

However, where office efficiency dictates, it may be desirable

[6] *Ibid.*

for the union to forego its usual drive to continually widen the scope of seniority units. Job or department units may have a useful role in the office. "Bumping" and rigid classification restrictions can result in higher costs in the office and technical fields than in the plant. The merits of such management arguments need to be objectively evaluated by the union on a situation-by-situation basis.

There is little disagreement among white-collar workers concerning layoff policies. Seniority is overwhelmingly approved as the fair criterion here. In interviews, however, there was a tendency for white-collar workers to accept more flexibility concerning the length of the probationary period.

In regard to promotion decisions, the union tendency to take the easy way out—by ridiculing the practicality of a merit program—appears particularly short-sighted where technical and professional workers are concerned. As Kassalow points out, a commitment to merit is "part of their professional identification." The union needs to seek a system in which merit can operate with fair objectivity.[7]

Merit appears to be an especially crucial issue among engineering groups. If, as may well be true, technicians can only be broadly organized after a breakthrough on the engineering front, then the imperative need for institutional flexibility and innovation by the union here is clear.

The Union Shop?

Experimentation with a less doctrinaire policy on union security may also be useful. The issue was sharply pointed out by the UAW's resoundingly publicized initial defeat in aerospace industry union shop elections in 1962.[8]

A willingness to moderate what appears to outsiders to be a union leadership obsession with security can contribute to a greater white-collar acceptance of unionization. The element of

[7] Harold J. Gibbons, Everett M. Kassalow, and Joel Seidman, "Developments in White-Collar Unionism," *Occasional Papers, No. 24* (Chicago: University of Chicago Industrial Relations Center, 1962), p. 9.

[8] *Labor Relations Reporter,* November 5, 1962, pp. 234–235, and November 12, 1962, p. 248.

compulsion in union shop provisions is often rejected by higher white-collar groups. Milder forms of union security—such as the agency shop arrangement or maintenance-of-membership clauses —might confer a necessary minimum membership stability. Some variety here would help to avoid highly unfavorable implications of union rigidity and "levelling."

In many instances, white-collar units ultimately move toward increasing support for stronger union security measures. However, in professional units a somewhat greater than traditional degree of membership "openness" might be practical even in the long run. For example, the independent Ford technicians organization, the Fraternity of Laboratory Workers, has survived for twenty-five years without any type of security provision. In this connection, the Electrical Workers' 1967 settlement with Sperry Rand is interesting. The union shop provision applied to those earning below $14,000, the agency shop to those above $14,000.[9]

The strength of white-collar feeling on this issue is illustrated by the reaction of Minneapolis-Honeywell employees to the statement, "If the majority of workers in a plant vote to have a union, the others should be required to join." Nearly two-thirds of the engineers and technicians disagreed with the statement, in contrast to only 4 percent of blue-collar union leaders and 15 percent of the rank-and-file members of other unions.[10]

Political Action

The UAW's activity in the arena of public politics is perhaps the most extensive—and effective—of any international or national union in the United States. There is a distinct public identification of the Union's interests with the Democratic party. It is clear that the political gains achieved and the "investment" of the Union in this program are both extensive and highly valued by the Union and its leadership. What implications does such a political program have for industrial union white-collar activity

[9] *White-Collar Report*, no. 536, June 15, 1967, pp. A-7 to A-8.
[10] See *Report of Findings on Attitudes, Communications and Participation of the Minneapolis Federation of Honeywell Engineers, Minneapolis, Minnesota, August, 1956* (Minneapolis: University of Minnesota Industrial Relations Center), Item 22.

generally? What modifications may prove desirable or necessary here?

The outer limits of the potential conflict are suggested by noting that the previously cited study of Minneapolis-Honeywell technicians and engineers found only 17 percent of interviewees agreeing with a statement, "I would not vote for a political candidate who was opposed by my union."[11] In the present study, a similar attitude was manifest, although results here were moderated by the exclusion of professional engineers. This view was also corroborated by a UAW team reporting on European white-collar union experience: white-collar membership tends toward somewhat greater conservatism in political matters.[12]

Kay Smith, in a study of Detroit-area automobile draftsmen, concluded that the predominantly negative attitudes toward unionism which he found among draftsmen were "a result of a combination of a general satisfaction with life and the job, identification with companies and management, and a general conservatism, both personal and political."[13] In view of these findings, it appears that the industrial union should avoid presenting a "radical" posture in its political policy statements and proposed programs. On the other hand, I found many elements of the UAW's present political program to be desirable or acceptable to white-collar workers.

Endorsement of Candidates

The primary liability of union political action for white-collar organizing does not center on the specific political program or

[11] *Ibid.*, Item 36.

[12] This mission's report represents one of the most constructive studies undertaken by the UAW in its approach to the white-collar problem. See Victor Reuther, Robert Shebal, and Irving Bluestone, "Report on Special Mission to Selected European Countries to Study White-Collar Worker Organization, March 16–April 10, 1959" (Detroit: International UAW-AFL-CIO, July, 1959), pp. 39–41.

[13] Kay H. Smith, "A Psychological Inquiry into Attitudes of Industrial Draftsmen toward Unionism" (Ph.D. dissertation, Wayne State University, 1961), p. 156.

lobbying activities of the union. Rather, the potential controversy revolves around the union's endorsement of candidates for public office. Here white-collar workers appear much less willing to accept the union's role of defining who shall be "our man." The slightest implication of being told how to vote is rejected.

The white-collar worker places a high value upon objectivity and independence of voting behavior. He is very conscious of the injunction to listen to both sides and to exercise individual judgment in making his political choices. Thus the union must afford a forum for conflicting views and conscientiously extend platform rights to opposing candidates. Emphasis upon membership participation in the endorsement process is also useful.

A realistic assessment of the political action issue seems to be that, in the future, if white-collar membership is increased, the industrial union will have a somewhat more difficult job in convincing its own members of the correctness of its basic political position. However, there is no sound basis for believing that there would be any revolt against the union's present program. The problem promises to be that of somewhat greater abstention and apathy on political issues—characteristics which also affect unions' present predominantly blue-collar membership. In this situation union political appeals, to be effective, would need to be increasingly objective and more carefully phrased and reasoned if they are to persuade the neutral or mildly disagreeing white-collar group.

In this study there was evidence that the UAW's political program was not a key issue in relation to white-collar organizing. It appeared that the Autoworkers' known preference for, and support of, Democratic candidates had only a slightly greater deterring effect among white-collar workers than it had with blue-collar workers in organizing campaigns. In terms of large-scale political strategy, industrial unions may gain a net advantage by incorporating white-collar members. Through the organizational structure and its communications channels these groups become more accessible for education and persuasion than when on the outside.

Spotlight on the White Collar

Jack Barbash emphasizes the white-collar worker's desire for high visibility in his union efforts.[14] Such visibility can also continually highlight the problem facing the union, and it can likewise perform a valuable educational function in relation to the blue-collar membership.

Thus, to the extent that internal political considerations permit, the International officers of an industrial union might well consider how they could best use their position at union functions to deliberately spotlight the white-collar group. They must be constantly aware of the need to support and express approval for white-collar participation in the institutional life of the union. A disproportionate white-collar membership upon convention committees might be encouraged in view of the importance of this group to the future of the union. In turn, at white-collar events those blue-collar union leaders who are most compatible with white-collar values might well be featured to symbolize the varied competence of the union's leadership.

As an industrial union's white-collar membership grows, there is a steadily increasing need for its leadership to interpret and mediate between white- and blue-collar groups. This parallels the requirement for external cooperation, as Sturmthal suggests: "Trade-union leaders may have to show unusual imagination and tolerance if effective cooperation between the organizations of manual and white-collar workers is to be established and maintained."[15] In this, as in other areas, the top leadership role will become more demanding of political skill and ingenuity and can be fulfilled less by routine and stereotyped administration. This may require more concentration of leadership time

---

[14] Jack Barbash, "What's Ahead for Labor," *Addresses on Industrial Relations* (Ann Arbor: University of Michigan Bureau of Industrial Relations, December, 1960), p. 9.

[15] Adolf Sturmthal, "White Collar Unions—A Comparative Essay," in Adolf Sturmthal, ed., *White Collar Trade Unions* (Urbana: University of Illinois Press, 1966), p 392.

and effort within the union, rather than in external activities in the larger community.

The industrial union's top leadership will need to resolve difficult internal political problems, such as the need to subsidize the white-collar operation for an extended period of time on an expensive scale. It will need to recruit quality white-collar organizers and to settle intra-union jurisdictional conflicts concerning the allocation of new members.

The adequacy and rate of adaptation of the industrial union to the white-collar drift offers an intense challenge to internal political leadership. The entire union, including its highly valued established relationships with management, must be moved from a dominantly blue-collar present through a perhaps only transitional blue-collar–white-collar balance into a predominantly white-collar future.

An Inventory

Having moved from the level of the intangibles of leadership attitudes, ideology, and philosophy through general union policies, let us now consider a number of specific activities and programs. A need for stock-taking is such an instance. Many industrial unions have only the vaguest notion of the numbers, diversity, and location of their existing white-collar membership. They know little or nothing of the trends in that membership and the special conditions and influences acting upon it. A fundamental beginning point, then, is for the industrial union to establish a vantage point that will facilitate analysis and thereby advance the possibility of creating a realistic and workable program. This requires a detailed inventory of the existing white-collar situation within the industrial union.

To know just what the present white-collar membership is, where it is located, why it succeeded in establishing itself in particular areas, what situational factors seemed relevant in both successful and unsuccessful organizing attempts, and what current trends affect present white-collar membership levels—these kinds of answers would seem to be a minimum requirement for

any rational, well-aimed attempt at organizing in this very difficult area. The inventory process might involve as many of the
white-collar staff and key blue-collar leaders as practical. The
understanding and awareness generated between staff, local
leaders, and blue-collar leadership by such an analysis would be
very valuable. The UAW's internal reappraisal of white-collar
affairs in 1962 seems to have been something of this type of
inventory.

A logical follow-up would be to require staff members to sub-
mit periodic analytical reports to insure that the basic inventory
could be kept current and useful. As a part of this same self-
study the union can assess the capability of the available staff
and take steps to recruit quality individuals from the white-collar
local unions. In some instances additional training for the present staff might be indicated. In other situations reassignment to
more appropriate functions elsewhere in the union's structure
will be necessary.

The Industrial Union's Newspaper

An industrial union establishes vital contacts with potential
white-collar members through the newspaper which it publishes
primarily for blue-collar members. Wide dispersion of the publication through the plant, offices, and community projects the
union's image far beyond the boundaries of its existing membership. In view of this, a conscious awareness of the newspaper's
potential for improving the white-collar worker's view of the
union can yield substantial dividends when the union is ready
to begin specific organizing campaigns.

In the interests of unity and inter-group relations it is probably
preferable for an industrial union to continue to produce a single
publication for its entire membership. In the case of the UAW,
interviewees' suggestions for improvement of *Solidarity* did not
involve major policy changes in this regard.

With relatively little effort, much can be accomplished to
meet white-collar interests—for example, by giving somewhat
greater emphasis and space to white-collar affairs and personali-

ties. It seems doubtful whether such a change would arouse important opposition from rank-and-file blue-collar members. Admittedly, this shift in emphasis might impinge somewhat upon the traditional political prerogatives of blue-collar officers.

From the apparent inability of the UAW white-collar group to secure such changes from the staff of *Solidarity,* it may be inferred that a special white-collar staff member should be assigned full time to the publication. Or a liaison person might be appointed to work between the newspaper and the specialized white-collar department of the International Union. The function is of such central importance to long-run organizing, as well as to internal education, that inadequate performance here is extremely short-sighted and costly.

Regular white-collar features and departments in the union's newspaper would seem to be an obvious, productive change, although this has not yet been accomplished within the UAW. Special efforts to upgrade the physical attractiveness and overall appearance of the union's primary publication would be well worth the expense involved. A white-collar supplement or "make over" edition appealing especially to the white-collar membership would also be productive.

Beyond this, serious consideration should be given to introducing a higher quality of journalism in the writing and presentation of issues in most union publications. An emphasis upon greater objectivity, a sparing use of slanted language, and an attempt to at least acknowledge opposing views might reduce the negative impact of the propaganda which white-collar workers frequently recognize and protest. Changes such as these would, at the same time, be in accord with blue-collar membership trends toward higher educational levels.

The industrial union's newspaper assumes symbolic importance in the minds of the white-collar workers who are reached by it. The newspaper furnishes visible evidence of the degree to which the union can be viewed as congenial to white-collar values.

Although labor-management relations in the United States have been historically studded with violence, a continual flaunting of "the bloody shirt," although intended to strengthen the loyalty and resolve of blue-collar members, may well repel those portions of the white-collar market which the union seeks to enter. It is possible that a factual investigation of the actual effectiveness of this emphasis might make it feasible to eliminate this particular stumbling block.

Of course, every encouragement should also be given to the publication of white-collar local union newspapers of high quality. This alternative, however, will be practical only if amalgamated local unions of white-collar members become the primary form of administrative grouping.

Other Public Relations Programs

Solomon Barkin suggests that the attacks on unions require "highly sophisticated rebuttal." But the trade union movement on the whole "continues to rely on the simpler tools of communication." An International Labor Organization study group has also concluded that "traditional methods are not enough." Modern technology offers "unprecedented opportunities" for "teaching large numbers of workers more rapidly than heretofore."[16]

A very long-range and extensive program of education and preparation may be required for broad-based white-collar organizing success. Television, although expensive, is particularly well adapted to this purpose. A joint effort sponsored by several industrial unions or the Industrial Union Department of the AFL-CIO would be a practical solution. The concentration of technical and clerical white-collar workers in metropolitan areas suggests that this medium might be practical also in conjunction with area organizing campaigns by several international unions. The immediacy of television and its access to white-collar employees at home seem well suited to the union's purpose. Early UAW experiments with television in organizing in Syra-

[16] "Twelve-Nation ILO Parley: Labor Educators Spur Radio, TV Use," *AFL-CIO News* (Washington, D.C.), December 30, 1967, p. 7. Also see Solomon Barkin, *Decline of the Labor Movement* (Santa Barbara, Calif.: Center for the Study of Democratic Institutions, 1961), p. 59.

cuse, New York, in 1955 might be a point of departure for further experimentation.[17]

In the Detroit area past union efforts in television and radio have been more successful with white-collar workers than have its printed publications. Further upgrading could pay valuable dividends. An emphasis upon objectivity and a concern for the imagery and tone of the union's representatives and commentators are minimum essentials in an experimental program of this type.

Certain subjects suggest themselves for development in such an educational effort. Programs illustrating the reassuringly routine office functions and personnel of the union itself might be useful among unorganized clerical workers. Profile programs on present union white-collar members which emphasize the variety and range of occupations already unionized could shatter some stereotypes. Research and education activities of the union might be highlighted, as well as the characteristically white-collar personnel—often with academic credentials—found in many staff operations of the union. The wide-ranging community participation of union officers at all levels would be an impressive item for presentation to the white-collar audience.

For maximum reach, such programs would require in addition a talent for showmanship such as demonstrated by the Office and Professional Employees' Local 153 public relations program in the New York metropolitan area.[18]

Blue-Collar Relations

One of the difficult dimensions of the white-collar problem for industrial unions is to maintain constructive relations between the blue-collar and white-collar membership groups. Here the top leadership of the union must mediate in the interests of the union as a whole. However, part of the problem can only be

[17] See Carl Dean Snyder, "The Organizing Campaign at New Process Gear," Syracuse, New York, 1957.
[18] *White-Collar Report,* no. 533, May 25, 1967, p. A-6.

successfully met by the increased understanding, awareness, and cooperation of blue-collar local union leaders and rank-and-file members.

An important avenue by which part of the true character of the industrial union is inevitably revealed to white-collar workers is through the activities of the shop local union in the same firm. A tendency toward irresponsibility, a militancy unnecessarily accentuated for political purposes within the local union, a resort to violence in labor disputes, or the (seemingly inconsequential) expression of a lack of respect toward management in the behavior of blue-collar stewards, committeemen, and officers can have costly effects upon the attitudes of unorganized white-collar members. Thoughtless acts such as these can undercut any broad public relations program undertaken by the International Union.

At the eighteenth constitutional convention of the UAW, Delegate Norman Roth of International Harvester Local 6 pinpointed the problem:

> Quite often in our local union elections we beat each other's brains out trying to win office, and while doing so we influence the office and technical workers around us in a negative fashion . . . when they see a cat and dog fight they say, "I don't want any such mess" . . . the image we present will go a long way in helping them decide and determine as to whether or not they want to join a union.[19]

The union also needs an efficient system of reporting organizing opportunities which appear in firms where blue-collar local unions already exist. White-collar organizing openings are highly local and fleeting in nature. Accurate information is essential. Thus a periodic checking by white-collar staff with blue-collar local union officers in key locations is indicated.

In actual organizing campaigns considerable care and selection is required to secure the maximum assistance from the blue-collar unit. Sometimes the local union's contribution can best be made simply by reporting information and "the lay of the land" to organizers.

[19] See UAW, *Proceedings, 18th Constitutional Convention, Atlantic City, N.J.,* May 4–10, 1962, p. 484.

Integration?

Interview results indicated that, unless deeply buried, there was little significant white-collar feeling that blue-collar bargaining gains were threatening the clerical and technical employees' status and traditional social position. At least in the automobile industry, the wage differential issue appeared quiescent. Gains by blue-collar workers were seen as objectively and socially desirable; in fact, these gains were frequently interpreted as productive of comparable white-collar improvements, due to the tandem benefit policies of automobile management.

Against this background, then, it appears that other industrial unions similarly situated have some freedom to pursue efforts to ultimately bridge the gap between blue- and white-collar workers in industry through mechanisms permitting the upgrading of shop workers. Two examples of such programs can be cited. I do not know whether or not they were initially conceived as part of a long-term strategy.

I refer first to the UAW's bargaining demand which asked that hourly workers be given salaried status.[20] The second proposal of the UAW, that displaced blue-collar workers be given opportunities to "try out" for openings appearing in the white-collar occupations, appears also as potentially useful to white-collar organizing progress. Both require adequate interpretation to avoid possibly undesirable effects upon white-collar opinion.[21]

Over the long run such innovations as these may operate to minimize strains arising from the incorporation of disparate blue- and white-collar elements within a single organization.

Union Functions: Redirection and Reemphasis

The full adaptation of the industrial union to the white-collar drift will necessitate some imaginative redirection of some already well-developed union functions—for example, those of education, research, and organizing.

[20] See "For Job Security Convert Hourly to Salary," reprinted in *White-Collar Report,* no. 219, May 15, 1961, pp. C-1 to C-4.
[21] *White-Collar Report,* no. 264, March 29, 1962, pp. A-4 to A-5, C-1 to C-3.

Much of the possibility of union success in the white-collar field lies in an effective internal and external process of education. The presentation of the union's true characteristics to the white-collar public, opportunities for interaction between white- and blue-collar members in the context of discussion and issue exploration, and staff training at professional levels are promising areas for action. Although the UAW's educational program has been a positive feature of the Union's image in the eyes of white-collar workers and the general public, the Union has failed to capitalize upon this possibility. Its Education Department continues to ignore the potential opportunity here.

The Research Function

Several areas for systematic investigation and research by union research departments suggest themselves. Perhaps most basic is the development of a method and an instrument by which white-collar attitudes can be periodically surveyed to provide a continuing guide to internal policy and organizing strategy and tactics.

Attitude checks to ascertain the effectiveness of the union's promotion techniques with white-collar workers would be most useful. Studies of white-collar opinion in both successful and unsuccessful organizing campaigns might be conducted. A systematic inventory of those economic items of special interest to white-collar workers can serve as the foundation for constructing an attractive bargaining program for this group.

If research could find ways of modifying it to better meet white-collar criteria, the representation mechanism implicit in the grievance procedure might become, as UAW President Walter Reuther once commented, "the key to the whole psychological problem among white-collar workers."[22] Interview results indicated little interest in the prevailing grievance mechanism as an organizing asset. However, James Kuhn reports a situation in

---

[22] Walter P. Reuther, "An Address," *Labor Looks at the White-Collar Worker* (Washington, D.C.: Industrial Union Department, AFL-CIO, 1957), p. 8.

which engineers, once familiar with the process, found grievance handling to be "the mainstay of the union."[23]

In the short run, research on bargaining data, model contract clauses, and grievances with broad policy implications is also badly needed. UAW Local 889 has likewise suggested the importance of establishing some guidelines as to the proper limits of bargaining units.[24]

The Organizing Function

The placing of organizing as the final area for union concern is deliberate. White-collar organizing cannot be usefully considered apart from indispensable preparatory work both within and without the union.[25] Lacking some of the various kinds of logistical support which we have been discussing, the white-collar organizing problem can probably be accurately characterized as impossible.

Specifically, white-collar organizers have suggested that organizing techniques must emphasize a strongly individual approach, personal contact, "inside" organizing committees, and, in some situations, extensive home visits. Promises must be realistic.

In view of the differences in white-collar psychology, it is important to emphasize intelligent argument as contrasted with emotion in organizing campaigns. It follows that this ability should be prominent in prospective organizing personnel. Emotional factors are significant in motivating all types of change, but discretion and "middle-class" forms of handling these elements are indispensable for their effective use with white-collar workers.

[23] James W. Kuhn, "Success and Failure in Organizing Professional Engineers," *Proceedings of Sixteenth Annual Meeting* (Madison, Wis.: Industrial Relations Research Association, 1964), p. 208.

[24] Wallace Webber et al., "Analysis of the White-Collar Organizational Problem: Presentation before the UAW International Executive Board" (Detroit: UAW Local 889, January 20, 1960), pp. 25–26.

[25] Barkin, *Decline of the Labor Movement*, p. 74.

A Good Aim

White-collar employment as an organizing field is characterized by the uniqueness of each separate situation. A high premium rests upon precision of effort. A "scatter gun" approach has virtually no chance of succeeding. John W. Livingston, formerly director of organization of the AFL-CIO, has commented, "Organizing among white-collar workers calls for greater individual attention than was required for organizing industrial workers in the past. General appeals or exhortations are apt to be less effective; specific appeals developed around specific problems are more likely to produce a favorable response."[26] The organizer must depend upon the functioning of an effective in-plant committee to identify the significant issues and evaluate alternative means of exploiting such issues.[27]

At this point, UAW experience has developed some general guides to workable organizing principles and the identification of typically favorable situations. These have been discussed in some detail in Chapter Six; thus it is only necessary here to point out that these are very relevant as starting points for other industrial unions.

Union Functions: The Legal Department

Joint action by industrial union legal talent might be useful in relation to the white-collar organizing problem through a frequent rechecking of several aspects of National Labor Relations Board policy. Test cases designed to secure more favorable NLRB interpretations on problems of bargaining unit "erosion," subcontracting, "the unit appropriate" for white-collar bargaining, elections for professionals, and the definition of supervisory employees could minimize white-collar membership losses and serve to promote white-collar membership gains.

[26] John W. Livingston, "The Transitional World of the White Collar," *AFL-CIO American Federationist*, March, 1961, p. 9.

[27] For a useful discussion of the functions of the in-plant committee, see Edward S. Haines and Alan Kistler, "The Techniques of Organizing," *AFL-CIO American Federationist*, July, 1967, pp. 31–32.

A currently unlikely possibility but a goal for the future might well be the reopening of NLRB service to supervisory associations. Such organization appears to have been useful in European white-collar unionization.[28]

A Long-Run Opportunity

Industrial unions cannot realistically expect major gains in the professional occupations in the industries of their jurisdictions until after sizable blocks of office and technical workers have demonstrated the acceptability and usefulness of unionism for white-collar industrial employees. However, the industrial union should be preparing its position in relation to this further field of white-collar organizing. The union needs to realize and accept the reality of professionalism. A valuable service is possible if it will identify those features of professionalism which are genuine and those which are merely superficial. Despite the present vagueness of the concept of professionalism, it carries the possibility of either winning or losing the higher levels of the white-collar group. To decry or deny the reality of the concept may be psychologically pleasurable, but it is hardly functional to the type of problem-solving required throughout the white-collar field.

An eventual successful resolution of this dilemma by the American Federation of Teachers could prove instructive for the industrial unions. It is useful to observe the emphasis put upon this concept by the National Society of Professional Engineers in its efforts to counter the interest of engineers in collective bargaining.[29] More immediately, it should be noted that "professionalism" was one of the recurring themes appearing in the reasons given by members of the ill-fated Minneapolis Federation of Honeywell Engineers for their anti-union vote in the decertification defeat of the UAW in 1957.[30]

[28] Kassalow, "Occupational Frontiers of Trade Unionism," p. 193.

[29] Engineer-in-Industry Committee, *The Engineer in Industry in the 1960's —A Professional Program* (Washington, D.C.: National Society of Professional Engineers, 1961), pp. 131–143.

[30] See Everett Taft and Gregory P. Stone, "An Unpublished Study of the Voting Record and Attitudes of the Minneapolis-Honeywell Federation of

The design of organizational structures for professional as well as technical workers should be guided by Solomon Barkin's description of the goals of the professional union. It deliberately tries to "integrate the promotion of the economic interests of its members and their status as creative individuals with the advancement of their competence and of public appreciation for the importance of the profession to society. . . ."[31]

The Dimensions of Change

The experience of the UAW and the extension of those efforts in a number of promising directions add up to a sizable prográm for interested industrial unions. In the long run the cumulative impact of increasing white-collar participation in industrial unions can be of great significance to the future of the labor movement.

In summary, the solution of the white-collar organizing problem of the industrial unions is not impossible. The problem does not require that the industrial union cease being a union in order to qualify for white-collar approval. On the other hand, the successful solution of this problem by the industrial unions will require the best efforts and political skill—as well as demanding commitments of time and attention—by the unions' top leadership.

Meeting the white-collar challenge will also necessitate a substantial (but finite) expenditure of funds, a modification of union structure in some specific areas, changes in policy and practice as they apply to white-collar workers, and a steady union alertness to unique organizing opportunities within the context of external conditioning trends. From these ingredients industrial unions can create successful institutional adaptation.

Engineers Who Were Surveyed by Mail during the Month Following the National Labor Relations Board Decertification Election, May 8, 1957."

[31] Barkin, *Decline of the Labor Movement*, pp. 49–50. However, in a survey of members of the National Society of Professional Engineers, Richard Stimson found that attitudes toward collective bargaining and unionism were more closely related to attitudes toward job satisfaction than to the concept of professionalism. See *White-Collar Report*, no. 773, January 7, 1972, p. A-1.

The White-Collar
Future of
Industrial Unions

10

Until now the emphasis has been placed upon the internal
changes required of industrial unions if they are to meet the
white-collar organizing problem. The challenge can only be met
through the initiative of the industrial unions themselves. UAW
experience and analysis suggest that there is a wide area for
improvement which is within the immediate control of the individual union and its leadership. Much valuable time has been
lost by industrial unions to date by looking for favorable global
events and total solutions or panaceas which are, by their nature,
beyond the control of the union institution. One of the most
meaningful contributions of UAW experimentation in the white-
collar field is that it has conclusively demonstrated that internal
innovation can make a vital difference. Now let us briefly consider the larger social and economic context for industrial union
organizing efforts among white-collar workers.

Continuing Inhibiting Factors

Interview materials indicate that, aside from the general limiting factor of anti-union attitudes on the part of some white-collar
workers, the single most effective bar to white-collar organization is management's policy of granting tandem benefits—benefits extended to white-collar workers subsequent to, and at least
equivalent to, those economic gains negotiated by blue-collar
unions in industry. For example, 74 percent of the unorganized

white-collar automobile employees interviewed gave this reason for their lack of interest in unionization. This basic policy is frequently supplemented by an elaborate personnel relations program designed to minimize white-collar discontent—accompanied by a "fire squad" approach to meet specific union organizing attempts.

Recent UAW convention resolutions emphasize frequent antiunion efforts by management in the white-collar field, even though blue-collar units have developed good bargaining relationships in the same firm. Such opposition to organization is regarded by the Union as "an unfriendly act . . . not conducive to the maintenance of friendly collective bargaining relationships." The TOP Department urges union negotiators to "incorporate clauses into our contracts pledging that corporations with whom we have agreements will not resort to vicious antiunion, anti-employee tactics during union representation election campaigns."[1]

The concept was reiterated at the 1970 (and 1972) conventions with a resolution urging

> . . . that UAW bargaining committees negotiate 'mutual respect' clauses into UAW corporate contracts. These clauses would recognize the right of non-supervisory and non-management employees presently unrepresented to join appropriate UAW bargaining units, and the right of the UAW to encourage such organization. They should express the intent of the corporation to avoid active involvement in any such organizing campaigns, neither assisting or encouraging any UAW efforts in this direction nor opposing such efforts or taking any action, direct or indirect, to discourage such organization.[2]

Lack of determined blue-collar support for this vital goal was demonstrated by the withdrawal of this bargaining demand during the 1970 auto negotiations. However, this may eventually emerge as a decisive factor in furthering UAW organizing suc-

[1] See UAW, *Proceedings, 20th Constitutional Convention, Long Beach, Calif.*, May 16–21, 1966, p. 75.

[2] UAW, *Proceedings, 22nd Constitutional Convention, Atlantic City, N.J.*, April 20–25, 1970, p. 77, and *White-Collar Report*, no. 789, April 28, 1972, p. A-11.

cess in the future. A perhaps stronger informal understanding between trucking employers and the Teamsters' union may explain the superior white-collar organizing record of that group.

Through the implementation of this approach or a similar one, industrial unions may be able to achieve a significant improvement in their organizing position. Until existing bargaining power is mobilized to support rather than to inhibit organization (through the possibility of jeopardizing existing relationships), the full strength of the union will not be effective in achieving its organizing goals. In countering negative management reactions and in securing positive management acceptance of white-collar unionization, the blue-collar leadership must be willing to invest some of its bargaining "coin" for the long-run future welfare of the union itself. Once overt management opposition is neutralized, a much more rapid spread of unionization within industrial union jurisdictions can occur.

National Labor Relations Board Rulings

The net effect of the intricate web of administrative law which has developed through the rulings of the National Labor Relations Board on representation elections and unfair labor practices is to discourage new organization. Once they are organized, however, legal certification does aid in maintaining the stability of white-collar units.

Finally, among inhibiting factors union deficiencies can be identified as a major reason for the lack of white-collar organization. The outstanding characteristic of most unions on the organizing front during recent years has been lethargy. In the white-collar area this was true even of such progressive unions as the UAW until 1961.

The Alternative Possibility

Most industrial unions may fail to effect the changes or commit the resources necessary for success in the white-collar field. The white-collar challenge requires important, specific changes within the industrial union. These appear to be both possible and practical changes, but they are fundamental enough to require a high level of vigorous, imaginative leadership within the union. Considerable political skill is demanded of the leadership to explain the need for these changes and to secure the active support of the blue-collar membership.

Thus Kahn was perhaps overly optimistic in believing that the changes which are required of the industrial union will, in fact, be made.[3] If industrial unions fail to meet the problem, white-collar organization will only be delayed—not indefinitely deferred. White-collar unionization will then by-pass existing organizations. In such a case, the economy would see the growth of new "associations" to meet white-collar representation needs.[4] The white-collar worker would still eventually find an organizational form that could meet "his dual need for security and self-esteem."[5]

The recent emergence of significant, spontaneous, independent white-collar unionism at both Ford and General Motors may thus mark a decisive change in office and technical worker opinion. It is entirely possible that the growing popularity of collective action throughout American society is becoming an increasingly important influence in union organizing. Such a development implicitly holds the potential opportunity of ultimate affiliation with the UAW or other industrial unions. A move to facilitate such affiliation and to permit a high degree of autonomy to initially independent professional groups was taken by the UAW at its 1972 convention. In response to a potentially rich organizing opportunity at North American Rockwell Corporation near Los Angeles, the UAW moved toward further adaptation to the interests of professionals. The convention granted the

[3] Mark L. Kahn, "Contemporary Structural Changes in Organized Labor," *Proceedings of Tenth Annual Meeting* (Madison, Wis.: Industrial Relations Research Association, 1958), p. 179.

[4] See Frederick C. Klein, "White-Collar Blues: Salaried Workers Find Cherished Job Security Is a Thing of the Past," *Wall Street Journal*, June 23, 1971, pp. 1, 29.

[5] The phrase is that of Roscoe Born in "Industrial Unions Fear Automation Will Cut Membership and Power," *Wall Street Journal*, April 7, 1959, pp. 1, 4.

International Executive Board the power to "take whatever action is required, including interim constitutional changes" to bring professionals into the Union either individually or in groups. Previous announcements by the National Engineers and Professionals Association (at NAR) had outlined an apparently new "affiliate status" in its relationship to the firm's production and maintenance local union, as well as an agreement stating the International Union's intent to form a specialized professional division. A breakthrough by the NEPA in the engineering field could well give the UAW the foothold among professionals that it missed by the loss at Minneapolis-Honeywell in 1957.[6]

It should also be noted that older professional associations are steadily moving toward taking on collective bargaining functions.[7] Additionally, the alternative possibility exists that, given enough time, the Office and Professional Employees' union is capable of absorbing at least the clerical workers in the industrial area.[8]

Craft or Industrial Unionism

Except in the professional occupations, any type of craft organization of white-collar workers in industry seems unworkable. However, various observers have examined the possibility.

[6] See *White-Collar Report,* no. 780, February 25, 1972, p. C-1, and no. 789, April 28, 1972, p. A-11.

[7] Terry F. Brown, "Organization Drive: Ired by Unemployment, the Nation's Engineers Move toward Unionism," *Wall Street Journal,* February 22, 1972, pp. 1, 14.

[8] One of the possible limitations upon the expansion of UAW white-collar membership in the industries of its jurisdiction is the conflicting claim of the Office and Professional Employees International Union (OPEIU) to these same workers. The craft-oriented OPEIU was granted charter jurisdiction by the AFL over office employees in the private sector of the economy, with the exception of the railroad industry. Prior to the 1955 AFL-CIO merger, unions in the Congress of Industrial Organizations had already maintained that these same workers were legitimately included within their respective industrial jurisdictions. The resulting tangle remained unresolved under the merger agreement. Section 2(c) of that agreement stated that "each affiliated union shall have the same organizing jurisdiction in the merged federation as it had in its respective prior organization." This was confirmed in the subsequent adoption of the AFL-CIO's constitution. See *Proceedings of the Seventeenth Constitutional Convention of the Congress of Industrial Organizations, New York, N.Y.,* December 1–2, 1955, pp. 270, 278.

In 1961 AFL-CIO Industrial Union Department Research Director Everett Kassalow gave explicit public backing to the industrial union form of white-collar organization. This led to protests by the Office Employees' union and the American Federation of Technical Engineers. The office group subsequently withdrew from the IUD.[9]

Kassalow maintained that it seemed improbable that the craft structure could be effective in American industrial bargaining circumstances. Power tends to follow corporate lines. Union history has demonstrated the indispensability of bargaining with corporate management from a united industrial union base.[10] In direct contrast, Jack Barbash has held that white-collar unionization must necessarily evolve toward some form of craft organization.[11]

John Livingston, AFL-CIO Director of Organization, in 1957 attempted to mediate between the two alternatives. He summarized the respective advantages as follows. In the industrial union the minority position of the white-collar group is strengthened by the bargaining support of the production worker members. The production local union is familiar with the industry and the tactics of its management and can thus offer useful bargaining counsel. In corporations organized by the industrial unions, the achievements of unionism are familiar to the office workers; this can encourage organization. On the other hand, in the all–white-collar union, the minority bargaining position can be alternatively protected through cooperation with the production worker local. Specialists in white-collar problems and needs can handle the interests of such workers more effectively. Unorganized white-collar workers will more easily accept union-

[9] As recently as June, 1967, the OPEIU has contended that there should be "one giant white-collar union for white-collar workers." See *White-Collar Report*, no. 537, June 22, 1967, p. A-1.

[10] Everett M. Kassalow, "Occupational Frontiers of Trade Unionism in the United States," *Proceedings of Thirteenth Annual Meeting* (Madison, Wis.: Industrial Relations Research Association, 1961), pp. 202–203.

[11] Jack Barbash, "What's Ahead for Labor," *Addresses on Industrial Relations* (Ann Arbor: University of Michigan Bureau of Industrial Relations, December, 1960), pp. 10–13.

ism when it is proposed by an exclusively white-collar group.[12]

However, in my opinion the establishment of completely new organizations for white-collar workers would be highly wasteful of social resources already invested in the existing industrial union structure. Adaptation seems preferable to duplication. The craft approach would slow the already overdue process of establishing adequate forms of representation for the increasingly numerous white-collar components of the labor force, and it would introduce unnecessary disruption of industrial production deriving from lack of experience and the splintering of negotiations in industry.

In addition, completely independent organization of white-collar workers would act to perpetuate the social class gap between blue- and white-collar groups. Such a development would introduce permanent obstacles to the most effective coordination of employee efforts in areas of mutual concern in the economic, social, and political arenas.

For the trade union movement such organization would be deleterious in ways similar to those following from the split in the labor movement in the 1930's. "The great hope today is that the essential changes can be made without schism—by evolution rather than revolution."[13]

In the 1966 UAW convention, debate on the constitutional change to permit separate voting by skilled trades, production workers, and other groups on contract ratification hit the issue squarely. President Reuther stated:

> That is the lesson that we need always to keep in mind: that no craft union ever organized General Motors. They had 50 years, and they got nowhere. And the production workers got nowhere alone. We won only when we put together that invincible power of a united industrial approach in which skilled-trades workers and production workers, while they obviously have

[12] See John W. Livingston, "The Answer for the White-Collar Worker," *Labor Looks at the White-Collar Worker* (Washington, D.C.: Industrial Union Department, AFL-CIO, 1957), pp. 67–68.

[13] Solomon Barkin, *Decline of the Labor Movement* (Santa Barbara, Calif.: Center for the Study of Democratic Institutions, 1961), p. 67.

different problems, nevertheless, brought to bear upon the collective bargaining process their combined leverage.[14]

Trends Favoring Unionization: Convergence

A fundamental long-term advantage of the industrial union approach lies in the trend toward greater homogeneity in the social characteristics of the labor force in the United States. The historically sharp differentiation between white- and blue-collar workers is slowly being eroded by the increasing educational level of the blue-collar portions of the labor force and the emergence of "middle-class" characteristics in the membership of the industrial union. On the other hand, some white-collar jobs have moved toward semi-industrial qualities. Differences will exist and be significant for many years, but the basic movement toward homogeneity will help to integrate the two primary occupational groups within a common organizational framework.

W. Donald Wood mentions the decreasing gap between manual and lower-level white-collar workers, and he suggests that a number of management and union policies are still "geared to the thirties and are often out of touch with this new work force."[15] William Kircher, director of the AFL-CIO Department of Organization, also stresses that the worker ". . . who has completed just over four years of high school today is not the same as the worker who had one year of high school education in 1940."[16]

These changes have been accompanied by increasing involvement of younger laborers with the techniques and attractiveness of collective action in the 1960's. This background may ultimately prove of decisive significance in relation to future white-collar organizing. Leonard S. Janofsky, in an address to the American Bar Association, argued that this trend would cause

[14] See UAW, *Proceedings, 20th Constitutional Convention,* pp. 412–413.

[15] W. Donald Wood, "White-Collar Unionism in Canada, 1967," Outline of presentation made to Shell Canada management course held at Queen's University Industrial Relations Center, June 5 to 23, 1967, p. 12.

[16] William L. Kircher, "Labor's Approach to the New Worker," *AFL-CIO American Federationist,* July, 1967, pp. 2–3.

semi-professionals and professionals to stop thinking that they are exempt from, or should be exempt from, collective bargaining. These young people "think differently than probably the bulk of the work force thinks now."[17]

In looking at other positive factors favoring unionization, probably the most significant long-term trend is the massive drift toward white-collar dominance in the labor force. Industrial unionism itself testifies to the tremendous drive for identity and recognition that arises in response to mass production pressures. Multiplication in numbers inevitably means increasing anonymity for the individual white-collar worker.

Increasing Insecurity

In the automobile industry the results of management concern for white-collar morale can be found in a relatively low level of employee job dissatisfaction. Interviews indicated at least a minimum sense of job security. However, it also appeared that an important minority of 30 to 35 percent of unorganized white-collar employees had experienced increasing work pressure, more frequent layoffs, and greater job insecurity.[18] A continuing trend in the direction of greater dissatisfaction is inevitable, in view of the increasing cost burden implicit in the shift of employment from blue- to white-collar occupations.[19]

In 1972 unprecedented unemployment among engineers created rising interest in collective bargaining as a means of achieving greater job security.[20]

Automation: "The Threat That Failed"

Automation is among the contemporary economic trends relevant to overall white-collar unionization possibilities. Initially,

---

[17] See Leonard S. Janofsky's remarks as reported in *White-Collar Report*, no. 703, August 28, 1970, pp. A-2 to A-3.
[18] Robert B. Cooney, "Loosening the White Collar," *AFL-CIO American Federationist*, July, 1967, p. 21.
[19] Klein, "White-Collar Blues," p. 29.
[20] Brown, "Organization Drive," pp. 1, 14.

automation seemed to contain a tantalizingly attractive organizing influence for the union. Its introduction into the office would provide the long-sought-for "automatic" solution to the organizing problem among clerical workers.

Although automation has had a significant impact upon office employment and its structure, the expected polarizing effect has not materialized. Management's careful attention to the displacement effects and companies' systematic utilization of attrition have kept personnel problems manageable without affording an organizing opportunity to the union.[21]

A Second Chance?

Nevertheless, it can be argued that an adequately prepared union can sometimes identify specific organizing openings where installations of automatic equipment are initiated. This is especially likely where routinization and shift work are introduced.

In 1972 automation had begun to affect employment opportunities and working conditions for technicians in the automobile industry.[22] Revolutionary changes in the technology of design were clearly in the making. An early estimate suggested that 20 percent of the duties performed by draftsmen and civil and electrical engineers could be performed by computers.[23] The materializing of such an influence upon the technical job market can, at some point, mean an important opening for union organization. Kay Smith mentions a flooding of the job market as one of the events which might be sufficient to reverse the antiunion sympathies of draftsmen in the Detroit area.[24] By 1972 a significant drive to unionize architectural employees had begun in this very group.[25] Another study suggests that ". . . there is

[21] Albert A. Blum, *Management and the White-Collar Union* (New York: American Management Association, 1964), p. 64.

[22] See *White-Collar Report*, no. 784, March 24, 1972, p. A-4.

[23] P. J. McGovern, "Probable Effects of Automatic Computers on the Professions," *Computer and Automation*, July, 1960, pp. 14–16.

[24] Kay H. Smith, "A Psychological Inquiry into Attitudes of Industrial Draftsmen toward Unionism" (Ph.D. dissertation, Wayne State University, 1961), p. 170.

[25] Ralph Orr, "New Union Is Attracting Architects and Engineers," *Detroit Free Press*, March 12, 1972, p. 17-D.

general agreement that it will be technically feasible to significantly reduce the number of draftsmen needed by industry within
20 years."[26]

The possibilities for complementarity should also be noted.
An accelerated pace of equipment development is probable.
Lowered equipment costs and greater equipment flexibility are
in prospect. The steadily increasing and pervasive pressure of
the cost burden of white-collar employment encourages the sub-
stitution of equipment for labor. Everett Kassalow points out:
"It is one thing to treat such workers as set costs when they constitute 10 or 15 per cent of total payroll, but possibly quite another when they reach 25 or 30 per cent or more."[27]

The "Costs of Nonorganization"

In the automobile industry, white-collar local union leaders have
raised an interesting hypothesis. They argue that the extension
of white-collar organization to General Motors and Ford may
finally occur, paradoxically, upon the basis of primarily economic
advantages to those companies. The "costs of nonorganization"
for the nonunion portion of the industry are steadily mounting.
Management's strategy of granting tandem benefits (as well as
having to meet the more visible gains of organized Chrysler
white-collar workers) means that a substantial portion of the
costs that would arise from white-collar unionization are already
unavoidably incurred. These costs would not be increased by
actual unionization. On the other hand, however, it is probable
that the unorganized companies presently enjoy substantial sav-
ings in *average* salary differentials.

Offsetting the latter advantage is the fact that the unorganized
companies must carry the heavy cost of constant readiness to
counter specific union organizing thrusts. To do so requires an
extensive permanent staff devoted to "improving supervision"
with the objective of avoiding unionization. Seniority patterns

[26] "Technology and Manpower in Design and Drafting, 1965–1975," *Man-power Research Bulletin, No. 12*, October, 1966, p. 38.

[27] See Everett M. Kassalow, "White-Collar Unionism in the United States,"
in Adolf Sturmthal, ed., *White-Collar Trade Unions* (Urbana: University of
Illinois Press, 1966), p. 358.

must be fairly closely followed, as though the company were already unionized. Some extra allowance for white-collar job continuity during business slumps may also be advisable.

All of these factors tend to freeze expenditures for white-collar services into a fixed cost pattern. At the same time technology steadily increases the proportion of the working force in the white-collar classifications. Thus, in certain respects, the advantage of freedom of movement actually lies with the organized Chrysler Corporation!

Faced with these trends, Ford and General Motors managements may at some point ask, "What do we gain in return for the high costs of maintaining a white-collar 'open shop'?" Are such intangibles as management pride in the undivided "loyalty" of its white-collar workers, and a partly illusory flexibility in the use of the working force, worth the very real costs of anti-unionism? If the open-office automobile companies once conclude that the answer is negative, a rapid union coverage of white-collar workers in these firms is highly probable. This might easily follow a pattern similar to Ford's acceptance of blue-collar unionism.

In support of this possibility it might be noted that a University of Michigan study of management representatives found some of the relevant questions already being asked. Thus a few managers expressed apprehension over the "anticipated cost and tension of successfully meeting a never-ending union challenge." It was suggested that a vicious circle had developed. The union kept raising its ante of promises. In consequence, the company was forced to spiral salaries and benefits to increasing new highs in order to keep its clericals from bargaining collectively through a union.

A very clear statement of the possible management shift in the future was included in one manager's comment: "If in the future our white-collar employees want to join a union, why fight it? In the long run it's more economical and a lot easier on the ulcers than playing a game of cat and mouse."[28] In qualifica-

[28] See Clark Caskey, "White-Collar Employees—A Union Dilemma and a Management Challenge," (Ann Arbor: University of Michigan Bureau of Industrial Relations, 1962), pp. 12–13.

tion, however, it should be pointed out that the study indicated that this view was definitely a minority attitude.

Supplemental Considerations

The likelihood of the "costs of nonorganization" hypothesis may be increased by two supplemental tendencies. One of these is the inclination of management to underestimate the significance of the equal benefits policy in shaping white-collar attitudes. In my interviews unorganized white-collar employees placed this practice near the top in giving reasons for not needing to unionize, but management representatives tended to see other factors as more important. In conjunction with increasing white-collar cost pressures this contrasting evaluation could lead to a weakening management commitment to the tandem benefits policy and a resultant opening for unionization.

Second, management is giving increasing consideration to methods of reducing its white-collar staff. Methods changes and analysis of companies' white-collar operations are recommended by business publications. A prominent *Wall Street Journal* article spotlighted the tendency in the early 1960's. The final instance cited had special relevance for the present discussion.

> One of the most rigorous belt-tightening operations by a major corporation was undertaken by Chrysler Corporation in 1961. It fired 7,000 of 36,000 white-collar employees, from secretaries to high-ranking executives. The action helped lower Chrysler's break-even point to 725,000 cars and trucks from a million units. President Lynn A. Townsend says the cutback didn't impair efficiency.[29]

Concern for the effects of such a cutback upon white-collar attitudes toward unionism at Ford and General Motors must be an important inhibiting element in pursuing a similar policy.

[29] Albert R. Karr, "White-Collar Cutback," *Wall Street Journal,* January 3, 1963, pp. 1, 14.

The Teachers Set an Important Example

The 1961 victory of the American Federation of Teachers, AFL-CIO, in the highly strategic and nationally prominent New York public school system was a historic turning point in the unionization of white-collar employees in America.

Subsequent AFT successes in other major cities have renewed the vitality of local chapters across the nation and have produced a sharp jump in membership and a fundamentally changed image of the white-collar worker's relation to the labor movement. The community and social acceptability of white-collar unionism has been importantly advanced. Teachers are typically "white collar"; their occupational prestige equals that of technicians in industry and is often superior to that of workers in clerical positions. If the National Education Association eventually accepts affiliation with the AFL-CIO, another major boost to white-collar organizing will occur.

Public Employee Unionism

The rapid expansion of organization among other government employees (both federal and state) is also a significant contributor to accelerating white-collar unionization. Interestingly, the white-collar portion of federal unions outside the postal service increased at a much more rapid rate than "gray" and "blue" segments between 1964 and 1966.[30] The full effects of President Kennedy's historic Executive Order 10988 have still to be realized, but the trend to date has been clearly favorable to white-collar unionization. In 1968 white-collar workers constituted over 40 percent of government union members.[31]

In those states where specific legislation to support collective bargaining by public employees has been enacted (as in Michigan in 1965), the climate for white-collar organizing has be-

[30] See "Labor-Management Relations in the Public Service," *Monthly Labor Review*, July, 1967, pp. iii–iv.

[31] See U.S. Bureau of Labor Statistics, *Directory of National and International Labor Unions in the United States, 1969* (Washington, D.C.: U.S. Department of Labor, 1970), p. 71.

come distinctly more favorable. It should also be noted that an adjacent, transitional group, employees of nonprofit employers, is likewise showing an active interest in unionization.[32]

A UAW Take-Off Point?

Analogies are perilous analytical devices. But it might be noted that the UAW, alone among industrial unions, has accumulated a bloc of some 88,000 white-collar unionists. This was about the size of the base from which the Teachers' union, with some assistance from other unions, began a rapid expansion of its membership despite the determined competition and opposition of the huge National Education Association.

With the UAW white-collar group's growing ability to influence policy within the Union and to operate more effectively in organizing, it seems reasonable to ask whether the UAW is at, or closely approaching, a critical take-off point in relation to white-collar unionization in its jurisdiction. UAW success could make possible a major breakthrough for other industrial unions. It would then be imperative for the industrial unions to embark upon a program that would permit them rapidly to exploit the organizing momentum that UAW success could establish.

The Impact of White-Collar Unionism on the Economy

Turning from the problems and prospects facing industrial unions to the more general implications of the white-collar unionization trend for the entire economy, certain possibilities should be briefly cited. I conclude that the organization of white-collar workers—preferably by the industrial unions, but alternatively in entirely new white-collar associations—is socially desirable. This evaluation is in accord with the long-standing public policy in support of collective bargaining as enunciated in the Wagner Act and subsequently reaffirmed in the Taft-Hartley Act.

Attempts to preserve individual bargaining as a method of

---

[32] Jack Golodner, "Unions and Non-Profit Employers," *AFL-CIO American Federationist,* August, 1970, pp. 19–24.

resolving the conflict of interest between employer and employee (despite a rising flood of millions of white-collar employees) seem highly unwise. In such situations individual bargaining is inherently limited to the salary item. As Sanford Lenz of the Electrical Workers' union points out, all other conditions of employment, such as insurance, pensions, leave, vacations, and holidays, "are determined by corporate policy which permits little room for individual deals."[33] The implicit management paternalism and the voicelessness of white-collar workers under a tandem benefits philosophy is seldom clarified. White-collar workers are thus denied genuine representation.

Even broader social considerations are involved. Fritz Croner argues that, if the more and more important white-collar group is not integrated into the structure of modern industrial society, "the rapid social developments of our time can easily place too great a strain on the structure and cohesion of our society."[34] In a similar direction, Adolf Sturmthal indicates that white-collar workers gave substantial support to Hitler's rise.[35]

If the influence of existing unions were eventually weakened to ineffectiveness by the white-collar drift, it is hard to see how the unions' indispensable countervailing functions in the economic, social, and political realms could be replaced. Thus Solomon Barkin maintains, "Trade unions are essential to an effective decentralized, pluralistic, democratic society. If they are weakened, the base for this society is itself weakened."[36]

Implications for Management

Not only are unions for white-collar employees socially desirable, in the broadest sense, but I found no evidence that management was unable to adapt successfully to their presence. Fair or good relations were reported frequently by both parties.

[33] *White-Collar Report,* no. 563, December 21, 1967, p. A-3.
[34] See Fritz Croner, "Salaried Employees in Modern Society," *International Labour Review,* February, 1954, p. 109.
[35] Adolf Sturmthal, "White-Collar Unions—A Comparative Essay," in Sturmthal, ed., *White-Collar Trade Unions,* p. 385.
[36] Barkin, *Decline of the Labor Movement,* pp. 64–66.

Other authors report similar conclusions. An extensive study of office unionization has stated that "nearly sixty-four percent of the companies reported . . . that the union has had no effect on the overall efficiency (of the office)."[37] Thompson and Weinstock report "a strong and widespread support for unions" in the Tennessee Valley Authority that derives from positive management encouragement.[38]

In a particularly crucial white-collar area, engineering, one analyst has commented that "management's reaction to the engineering union is largely an emotional one. . . ." Where engineering unions existed, there were some mutual gains recorded. Some of the fears concerning the alleged influence of unionization toward mediocrity, minimum performance, nonprofessionalism, and diminished creativity were found to be "thus far largely unfounded." The study suggested that engineering unions have characteristics distinctly different from shop unions. If they are treated differently by management, these unions can also have quite different effects within the business organization.[39]

The Quality of Relationships

In my examination of white-collar unionization in the automobile industry, there was strong evidence from both active unionists and management representatives that good relationships were entirely feasible and had, in fact, developed in many instances. Table 10–1 presents the data derived from interviews with active unionists.

Despite strong company opposition to initial white-collar organization, a workable and often relatively cordial relationship can eventually evolve between organized white-collar workers and management. This conclusion is supported by the interview data in Table 10–2.

[37] See *Daily Labor Report*, no. 22, February 2, 1961, p. B-3, for this survey by the National Office Management Association.

[38] Arthur Thompson and Irwin Weinstock, "White-Collar Employees and the Union at TVA," *Personnel Journal*, January, 1967, pp. 14–21.

[39] Richard E. Walton, *The Impact of the Professional Engineering Union* (Boston: Harvard University Graduate School of Business Administration, 1961), pp. 355–356, 368–369, 377–379.

TABLE 10–1. ACTIVE WHITE-COLLAR UNIONISTS'
EVALUATION OF COMPANY-UNION RELATIONS

Question: How good are the relations of your white-collar
unit with the company?

Very good, cooperation on most problems	45%
Generally good, but some important disagreements	18%
Fair	27%
Very poor, continual conflict	9%

Most observers would agree that generally tolerable relationships exist between management and blue-collar employees in
the automobile industry. Thus it follows from the data in Table
10–2 that many management fears about the probable effects
of white-collar unionization are exaggerated. It will be noted
here that in nearly three-fourths of the instances reported the

TABLE 10–2. MANAGEMENT'S EVALUATION
OF COMPANY-UNION RELATIONS

Question: Are your labor relations with your unionized white-collar workers better or worse
than with your blue-collar group?

Better than with the shopworkers' unit	47%
The same as with the shopworkers' unit	26%
Worse than with the shopworkers' unit	27%

relationships were at least as good as those achieved with the
shop group. Significantly, the intermediate category ("the same
as shopworkers' unit") contained at least half of the instances
where the relationships were reported as "very good" with both
groups.

Conclusion

Industrial unions with quality leadership can successfully adapt
to the changing manpower characteristics of the labor force
through a realistic, practical program of internal change. Such
industrial union adaptation can offer broad social benefits for
American society. Actual white-collar collective bargaining experience also demonstrates that good relationships are entirely

feasible between organized white-collar employees and their employing corporations.

As a final word on the prospects for white-collar unionization, it seems appropriate to cite C. Wright Mills: "Freedom is, first of all, the chance to formulate the available choices, to argue over them—and then, the opportunity to choose. . . . The future of human affairs is not merely some set of variables to be predicted. The future is what is to be decided—within the limits, to be sure, of historical possibility."[40]

---

[40] As cited by Alvin W. Gouldner in "Anti-Minotaur: The Myth of a Value-Free Sociology," in Irving L. Horowitz, ed., *The New Sociology: Essays on Social Values and Social Theory in Honor of C. Wright Mills* (New York: Oxford University Press, 1964), p. 158.

Bibliography

Barbash, Jack. "What's Ahead for Labor." *Addresses on Industrial Relations.* Ann Arbor: Bureau of Industrial Relations, University of Michigan, 1960.

Barkin, Solomon. *Decline of the Labor Movement.* Santa Barbara, Calif.: Center for the Study of Democratic Institutions, 1961.

Barry, Carol. "Special Labor Force Report." *Monthly Labor Review,* January, 1961.

Beirne, Joseph. *New Horizons for American Labor.* Washington, D.C.: Public Affairs Press, 1962.

Blum, Albert. *Management and the White-Collar Union.* New York: American Management Association, 1964.

————, ed. *White-Collar Workers.* New York: Random House, 1971.

Brady, James T., et al. *Teamwork in Technology: Managing Technician Manpower.* Scarsdale, N.Y.: Technician Manpower Associates, 1959.

Bruner, Dick. "Why White-Collar Workers Can't Be Organized." *Harper's,* August, 1957.

Burgin, Phyllis. "Minutes of the First Annual T.O.P. International Conference." Detroit: UAW Technical, Office, Professional Department, March 22, 1967.

Burns, Robert K. "Unionization of the White-Collar Worker." *Personnel Series, No. 110.* New York: American Management Association, 1947.

Caskey, Clark. "White-Collar Employees—A Union Dilemma and a Management Challenge." Ann Arbor: Bureau of Industrial Relations, University of Michigan, 1962.

Cohany, Harry P. "Trends and Changes in Union Membership." *Monthly Labor Review,* May, 1966.

Cooney, Robert. "Loosening the White Collar." *AFL-CIO American Federationist,* July, 1967.

Croner, Fritz. "Salaried Employees in Modern Society." *International Labour Review,* February, 1954.

Cross, Ira B., Jr. "When Foremen Joined the CIO." *Personnel Journal,* February, 1940.

Dale, Ernest. *The Unionization of Foremen.* New York: American Management Association, 1945.

Danielson, Lee R. *Characteristics of Engineers and Scientists.* Ann Arbor: Bureau of Industrial Relations, University of Michigan, 1960.

Engineer-in-Industry Committee. *The Engineer in Industry in the 1960's—A Professional Program.* Washington, D.C.: National Society of Professional Engineers, 1961.

Evan, William M. "On the Margin—The Engineering Technician." *The Human Shape of Work.* Edited by Peter L. Berger. New York: Macmillan, 1964.

Foote, Nelson N. "The Professionalization of Labor in Detroit." *American Journal of Sociology,* January, 1953.

Friedman, Marvin. "The Changing Profile of the Labor Force." *AFL-CIO American Federationist,* July, 1967.

Gibbons, Harold J.; Kassalow, Everett M.; and Seidman, Joel. "Developments in White-Collar Unionism." *Occasional Papers, No. 24.* Chicago: University of Chicago Industrial Relations Center, 1962.

Goldstein, Bernard. "The Perspective of Unionized Professionals." *Social Forces,* May, 1959.

Gouldner, Alvin W. "Anti-Minotaur: The Myth of a Value-Free Sociology." *The New Sociology: Essays on Social Values and Social Theory in Honor of C. Wright Mills.* Edited by Irving L. Horowitz. New York: Oxford University Press, 1964.

Haines, Edward S., and Kistler, Alan. "The Techniques of Organizing." *AFL-CIO American Federationist,* July, 1967.

Hatt, Paul K., and North, C. C. "Prestige Ratings of Occupations." *Man, Work and Society.* Edited by Sigmund Nosow and William Form. New York: Basic Books, 1962.

Henig, Harry. *The Brotherhood of Railway Clerks.* New York: Columbia University Press, 1937.

Homans, George C. "Status among Clerical Workers." *Human Organization,* Spring, 1953.

Hoos, Ida R. *Automation in the Office.* Washington, D.C.: Public Affairs Press, 1961.

Indik, Bernard P., and Goldstein, Bernard. "Professional Engineers Look at Unions." *Proceedings of Sixteenth Annual Meeting.* Madison, Wis.: Industrial Relations Research Association, 1964.

Industrial Union Department, AFL-CIO. *Labor Looks at the White-Collar Worker.* Washington, D.C., 1957.

"Interview with VH on Society of Designing Engineers." Society of Designing Engineers—Organization and Administration. Brown Collection, Archives, Wayne State University Library.

Kahn, Mark L. "Contemporary Structural Changes in Organized Labor." *Proceedings of the Tenth Annual Meeting.* Madison, Wis.: Industrial Relations Research Association, 1958.

Kassalow, Everett M. "New Union Frontier: White-Collar Workers." *Harvard Business Review,* January–February, 1962.

Kircher, William L. "Labor's Approach to the New Worker." *AFL-CIO American Federationist,* July, 1967.

Kuhn, James W. "Success and Failure in Organizing Professional Engineers." *Proceedings of the Sixteenth Annual Meeting.* Madison, Wis.: Industrial Relations Research Association, 1964.

Lipset, S. M. "The Political Process in Trade Unions." *Freedom and Control in Modern Society.* Edited by Morroe Berger, Theodore Abel, and Charles Page. New York: Van Nostrand, 1954.

Livingston, John W. "The Transitional World of the White Collar." *AFL-CIO American Federationist,* March, 1961.

Lombardi, Vincent, and Grimes, Andrew. "A Primer for a Theory of White-Collar Unionization." *Monthly Labor Review,* May, 1967.

McGee, Reece. "White-Collar Explosion." *Nation,* February 7, 1959.

Madar, Olga M. "Letter to Officers and Delegates of the T.O.P. Advisory Councils." Detroit: UAW Technical, Office, Professional Department, March 24, 1967.

Miller, S. M. "Discussion." *Proceedings of Thirteenth Annual Meeting.* Madison, Wis.: Industrial Relations Research Association, 1961.

———. "The New Working Class." *The Blue-Collar World: Studies of the American Worker.* Edited by Arthur B. Shostak and William Gomberg. Englewood Cliffs, N.J.: Prentice-Hall, 1964.

Mills, C. Wright. "The Middle Classes in Middle-Sized Cities." *American Sociological Review,* December, 1946.

———. *White Collar: The American Middle Classes.* New York: Oxford University Press, 1951.

National Association of Manufacturers. *A Report to Management on Unionization of Salaried Employees.* New York: Industrial Relations Division, National Association of Manufacturers, 1958.

———. *Satisfying the Salaried Employee.* New York: Industrial Relations Division, National Association of Manufacturers, 1957.

"News Flash." Organizing Committee of Detroit Chapter 201, Society of Designing Engineers, June 8, 1938. Brown Collection, Archives, Wayne State University Library.

"News Flash." Society of Designing Engineers, FAECT-CIO, July 2 and July 16, 1941. Brown Collection, Archives, Wayne State University Library.

"News Release." UAW Publicity Bureau, February 7, 1938. Brown Collection, Archives, Wayne State University Library.

Northrup, Herbert R. *Unionization of Professional Engineers and Chemists.* New York: Industrial Relations Counselors, 1946.

"The Rebirth of Ford." *Fortune,* May, 1947.

Reuther, Victor; Shebal, Robert; and Bluestone, Irving. "Report on Special Mission to Selected European Countries to Study White-Collar Worker Organization, March 16–April 10, 1959." Detroit: International UAW-AFL-CIO, 1959.

Reuther, Walter P. "An Address." *Labor Looks at the White-Collar Worker.* Washington, D.C.: Industrial Union Department, AFL-CIO, 1957.

Riegel, John W. *Collective Bargaining as Viewed by Unorganized Engineers and Scientists.* Ann Arbor: Bureau of Industrial Relations, University of Michigan, 1959.

Roethlisberger, F. J., and Dickson, William J. *Management and the Worker.* Cambridge: Harvard University Press, 1942.

Sayles, Leonard R., and Strauss, George. *The Local Union.* New York: Harper and Row, 1953.

Seidman, Joel, and Cain, Glen G. "Unionized Engineers and Chemists: A Case Study of a Professional Union." *Journal of Business,* July, 1964.

Sexton, Brendan. "The Intellectual and Trade Unions." *Proceedings of Sixteenth Annual Meeting.* Madison, Wis.: Industrial Relations Research Association, 1964.

Shostak, Arthur B. *America's Forgotten Labor Organization.* Princeton: Princeton University Press, 1962.

————, and Gomberg, William, eds. *The Blue-Collar World: Studies of the American Worker.* Englewood Cliffs, N.J.: Prentice-Hall, 1964.

Smith, Kay H. "A Psychological Inquiry into Attitudes of Industrial Draftsmen toward Unionism." Ph.D. dissertation, Wayne State University, 1961.

Snyder, Carl Dean. "Industrial Unions Can Lose the Battle for the White-Collar Worker: The UAW as a Case in Point." D.S.Sc. dissertation, Syracuse University, 1964.

————. "The Organizing Campaign at New Process Gear." Unpublished study. Syracuse, New York, 1957.

Society of Designing Engineers. "There Was a Time." Detroit: Detroit Council, Society of Designing Engineers, n.d.

Solomon, Benjamin. "The Problems and Areas of Union Expansion in the White-Collar Sector." *Proceedings of Ninth Annual Meeting.* Madison, Wis.: Industrial Relations Research Association, 1957.

Solomon, Benjamin K., and Burns, Robert K. "Unionization of White-Collar Employees: Extent, Potential, and Implications." *Journal of Business,* April, 1963.

Stieber, Jack. *Governing the UAW.* New York: John Wiley and Sons, 1962.

Strauss, George. "Professionalism and Occupational Associations." *Industrial Relations,* May, 1963.

————. "White-Collar Unions Are Different!" *Harvard Business Review,* September–October, 1954.

Sturmthal, Adolf, ed. *White-Collar Trade Unions.* Urbana: University of Illinois Press, 1966.

Taft, Everett, and Stone, Gregory P. "An Unpublished Study of the Voting Record and Attitudes of the Minneapolis-Honeywell Federation of Engineers Who Were Surveyed by Mail during the Month Following the National Labor Relations Board Decertification Election, May 8, 1957."

Thompson, Arthur, and Weinstock, Irwin. "White-Collar Employees and the Union at TVA." *Personnel Journal,* January, 1967.

UAW Engineering-Technical-Office Detroit Area Caucus. "Organize the Unorganized." Detroit: UAW Local 412, n.d.

UAW Local 412. *Engineering Leader*. Detroit: UAW Local 412, 1957–72.

————. "Letter to All Delegates Attending UAW White-Collar Conference." Detroit: UAW Local 412, February 22, 1962.

UAW Local 889. *White-Collar News*. Warren, Michigan.

UAW Technical, Office, Professional Department. *UAW TOP Reporter*. Detroit: UAW Technical, Office, Professional Department.

United Automobile, Aircraft, and Agricultural Implement Workers of America. *Convention Proceedings*. Detroit: International UAW, 1937, 1941, 1942, 1943, 1946, 1947, 1949, 1951, 1952, 1957, 1961, 1962, 1964, 1966, 1968.

————. *Report of the President*. Detroit: International UAW, 1943, 1944, 1952, 1957, 1964, 1966, 1968.

————. *UAW Solidarity*.

United Steelworkers of America. "Office and Technical Workers—Now Is the Time." Pittsburgh, n.d.

————. "Office and Technical Workers—Your Key to a Better Future." Pittsburgh, n.d.

University of Minnesota Industrial Relations Center. "Report of Findings on Attitudes, Communications, and Participation of Honeywell Engineers." Minneapolis: University of Minnesota Industrial Relations Center, 1957.

U.S. Bureau of Labor Statistics, Department of Labor. *Directory of National and International Labor Unions in the United States*. Washington, D.C., 1962, 1968, 1970.

U.S. Department of Labor. *Manpower Report of the President*. Washington, D.C., 1970, 1971.

Walton, Richard E. *The Impact of the Professional Engineering Union*. Boston: Harvard University Graduate School of Business Administration, 1961.

Webber, Wallace, et al. "Analysis of the White-Collar Organizational Problem: Presentation before the UAW International Executive Board." Detroit: UAW Local 889, January 20, 1960.

White-Collar Report. Washington, D.C.: Bureau of National Affairs, 1957–72.

Whyte, William F. "Engineers and Workers—A Case Study." *Human Organization,* Winter, 1956.

William, Whiting. "Guarding the Goodwill of White-Collar Workers." *Factory Management and Maintenance,* December, 1944.

Wood, W. Donald. "White-Collar Unionism in Canada, 1967." Kingston, Ontario: Queen's University, 1967.

Index

Advisory councils: as coordinating structure, 88–90

Aerospace industry: white-collar unionization of, 53

Agricultural implement industry: white-collar unionization of, 53–54

Analytical framework of study, 133–134

Associations: as alternatives to organization by existing unions, 168

Attitudes of active white-collar unionists: relations with blue-collar members, 65; toward Chrysler strike (1958), 68; toward *Solidarity*, 74; differences from blue-collar workers, 118; differential emphasis on job security, 119; job dislikes, 119

Attitudes of inactive white-collar unionists: identification of differences from blue-collar workers, 121; identification with interests of company, 121; evaluation of job importance, 121; more favorable view of the UAW, 122; strongly favorable opinion of top UAW leadership, 123; belief in necessity of unions, 123; toward participation in selected union activities, 123–124; issue of merit vs. seniority in promotion, 126–127; the union shop, 127–128;

political activities of the union, 128–129; stock ownership plans, 129–130

Attitudes of unionized white-collar workers: as viewed by local union leaders, 115–116

Attitudes of unorganized white-collar workers: toward advancement, 22; differences from shop workers, 22; preferences in jobs, 22; reasons for choosing occupation, 22; identification with employers' interests, 23; view of job importance, 23; perception of union image, 23–24; evaluation of UAW, 24; changes desired in unions, 24; view of union leaders, 24; reaction to union political activity, 25; effects of union membership on prestige, 25; toward union publication, television, and radio, 25; toward craft union alternative, 26; support for unionization, 27; sources of job dissatisfaction, 173

Automation: effects on organizing of white-collar workers, 91–92, 172–175

Autonomy of white-collar union members: constitutional provision (1957), 61–62; rejection at Briggs, 67; executive board grant of right to, 85; emphasis on, 93–94

MY 27

GAYLORD   PRINTED IN U.S.A.

HD6515.A8 S57   c.1
Snyder, Carl Dean.   100106 000
White-collar workers and the U

3 9310 00004045 9
GOSHEN COLLEGE-GOOD LIBRARY